NAWAL EL SAADAWI

Nawal El Saadawi – Egyptian novelist, doctor and militant writer on Arab women's problems and their struggle for liberation – was born in the village of Kafr Tahla. Refusing to accept the limitations imposed by both religious and colonial oppression on most women of rural origin, she qualified as a doctor in 1955 and rose to become Egypt's Director of Public Health. Since she began to write over 25 years ago, her books have concentrated on women. In 1972, her first work of non-fiction, *Women and Sex*, evoked the antagonism of highly placed political and theological authorities, and the Ministry of Health was pressurised into dismissing her. Under similar pressures she lost her post as Chief Editor of a health journal and as Assistant General Secretary in the Medical Association in Egypt. From 1973 to 1976 she worked on researching women and neurosis in the Ain Shams University's Faculty of Medicine; and from 1979 to 1980 she was the United Nations Advisor for the Women's Programme in Africa (ECA) and Middle East (ECWA). Later in 1980, as a culmination of the long war she had fought for Egyptian women's social and intellectual freedom – an activity that had closed all avenues of official jobs to her – she was imprisoned under the Sadat regime. She has since devoted her time to being a writer, journalist and worldwide speaker on women's issues.

With the publication by Zed Books in 1980 of *The Hidden Face of Eve: Women in the Arab World*, English-language readers were first introduced to the work of Nawal El Saadawi. Zed Books has also published three of her previous novels, *Woman at Point Zero* (1983), *God Dies by the Nile* (1985), and *The Circling Song* (1989). Nawal El Saadawi has received three literary awards.

Searching

Nawal El Saadawi

Translated by Shirley Eber

Zed Books Ltd
London and New Jersey

Searching was first published in Arabic. It was first
published in English by Zed Books Ltd, 57 Caledonian Road,
London N1 9BU, UK, and 165 First Avenue, Atlantic Highlands,
New Jersey 07716, USA, in 1991.

Cover designed by Andrew Corbett.
Cover Illustration by Phyllis Mahon.
Typeset by CentraCet, Cambridge.
Printed and bound in the United Kingdom
by Cox & Wyman Ltd, Reading.

British Library Cataloguing in Publication Data

Sadawi, Nawal
Searching.
I. Title
892.736 [F]

ISBN 1-85649-008-4
ISBN 1-85649-009-2 pbk

Searching

Part One

That morning as she opened her eyes the felt a strange depression creeping in her veins; stinging ants seemed to be streaming into her heart, where they coagulated like a clot of blood and rubbed against the wall of her heart with the rise and fall of her chest whenever she sneezed, coughed or took a deep breath.

She rubbed her eyes, not understanding the reason for this depression. The sun was as bright as usual, its glowing rays penetrating the window-pane fell on to the wardrobe mirror, throwing a red flame on to the white walls. The leaves of the eucalyptus tree shimmered and quivered like shoals of little fish, and the wardrobe, clothes-stand, shelf – everything – was in its usual place.

She threw back the covers, jumping up, and went straight to the mirror. Why did she look at her face the moment she woke up? She didn't know, only she wanted to assure herself that nothing untoward had happened to her as she slept . . . that no white speck had perhaps crept from the white of her eye to invade the black pupil; that no spot had appeared on the tip of her nose.

In the mirror was the same face that she saw every day: brown skin, the colour of milky cocoa; a wide brow on which hung a lock of curly, black hair; green eyes each containing a small black kernel; a long straight nose, and a mouth.

She looked quickly away from her mouth. She hated it, for it was her mouth that spoiled the shape of her face, that ugly involuntary gap as though her lips should have grown more, or her jaw bones less. Whether the one or the other, her lips did not close easily, leaving a permanent gap through which showed prominent white teeth.

She pursed her lips and began to look at her eyes as she always did when trying to ignore her mouth. Her eyes had something in them, something that distinguished her from other women, as Farid used to say.

The name Farid reverberated in her head. The veil of sleep was suddenly lifted; she remembered with absolute clarity and absolute certainty what had happened the previous evening. Then she understood the reason for the depression that weighed on her heart: Farid had not kept their date last night.

As she turned from the mirror, the telephone on the shelf by the bed caught her eye. She hesitated for a moment, then walked over to the bed and sat down, staring hard at the phone. She put a finger in the dial to turn the five numbers, then withdrew her hand and laid it beside her on the bed. How could she call him when he had broken their date without apology? Had he broken it on purpose? Was it possible that he did not want to see her? That his love had ended? Had ended as everything ended, with or without reason? And since it had ended, what was the use of knowing why? Besides, was it possible for her to know the reason? She didn't even know why it had started. He used to say that he saw something in her eyes, something he did not see in the eyes of other women, something that distinguished her from other women.

She stood up and walked back to the mirror and again looked into her eyes, examining them closely, searching for that something, and she she saw two wide, white ovals in which floated two green discs, a small, black kernel in the centre of each. Eyes like any others, like those of a cow or a slaughtered rabbit!

Where was that something Farid saw? Which she herself had seen? Had seen more than once, inside those two green circles, something that shone out of them distinct and animated, something with a life of its own. Had it gone? How? She remembered neither how it had gone nor if it was from those two green circles it had appeared. Perhaps it had appeared from somewhere else? from her nose, from her mouth? No, not from her mouth, not from that ugly gap . . .

There was nothing there. She saw nothing appear from any of them. Farid had lied. Why? He lied like anyone else. What was so strange about that? Only Farid was not anyone. He was

4

different, different from others. How? She didn't know exactly. But there was something in his eyes that made her feel he was different. Yes, something in his eyes that she did not see in the eyes of other men, something that shone from his brown eyes, distinct and animated like something alive. What was it? She didn't remember, didn't know, but she had seen it, yes, she had seen it.

She pointed a finger at her eyes, hitting the mirror. She gave a start and looked at the clock. It was eight. Quickly, she turned from the mirror; it was time to go to the Ministry.

In front of the wardrobe she paused again, for the word 'ministry' had entered her nose with the very air, like a splinter of guilt. She tried to sneeze it out, but, as she breathed, the air thrust it down into her chest to lodge in the triangle beneath her ribs or, more exactly, the aperture that opened into her stomach.

She knew it would lodge there, graze in that fertile field, eating, drinking and swelling. Yes, it swelled every day and pressed its sharpness into her stomach, which often tried to eject it, contracting and relaxing its muscles to rid itself of all that lay deep inside. But the barb remained, stabbing the wall of her stomach like a needle, clinging with its teeth, like a tapeworm.

She went to the bathroom, feeling a chronic pain under her ribs; wanted to vomit, but couldn't. She leaned her head against the wall. She was ill, a real illness, not faked. She could not go to the Ministry.

Energy spread through her slender body and she turned back to the bed, jumping on to it and pulling up the cover. She might have closed her eyes and slept, but it occurred to her that she must telephone the head of department and excuse her absence.

She pulled the telephone towards her, lifted the receiver, then immediately replaced it, remembering that she had used up all her sick-leave. No illness could excuse her, not even death could give her a holiday. She might claim that every member of her family, one after the other, had died and that she alone remained alive; she was still in her thirties and the head of department would not readily believe the news of her death.

5

Once again, she dragged her sluggish body from the bed, pressing her fingers into her stomach. She shot a glance at the mirror as she passed, and then dressed. She went towards the door and, opening it, heard her mother's faint voice from the kitchen:

'Aren't you having any tea?'

'I don't have time.'

She went out, shutting the door behind her. In the crowded street her eyes were turned within herself and she saw nothing. She might have walked into somebody or a wall, but her feet moved of their own accord with perfect knowledge, stepping up on to and down from the pavement, avoiding a hole, side-stepping a pile of bricks, as if they had eyes.

They came to a standstill at the bus stop. The dense crowd of bodies jostled her; someone trod on her foot and almost crushed it, but she felt only a pressure on her shoe. She was aware that she was inside the bus only by the vibrations through her body and that curious smell. She didn't know exactly what it was; it was strange; she didn't know where it came from for it did not have a single source, neither the pits under arms nor the dark cavity of mouths nor the flakes of skin that clung to greasy hair.

Something sharp was pressing into her shoulder. She had sensed it before but ignored it since there were many pressures on her from all sides, so why particularly care about her shoulder? But an insistent voice hammered into her ear, like a nail: 'Tickets'. A light rain of spray hit her face. She opened her bag with trembling fingers, for the man glowered at her like a policeman apprehending a thief, muttering something about 'responsibility' and 'conscience'.

She felt her face flush, not because of those two words – alone and out of context they were meaningless – but all eyes were turned towards her, in each a strange look as if in their hearts they too felt accused. But because they knew they would not be punished they were full of secret malice towards the one on whom punishment had fallen.

But she stood accused and as long as she did so she had

6

relinquished all right to respect. Men's eyes took possession of her body the way they appropriated those of prostitutes. Something pushed her. She shrank into her coat, burying her head in its wide collar. Her feet barely touched the ground, delivering her body to the heaving wave of bodies heading for the door. For a fleeting moment she was conscious of violent pressure, like a leaf or a butterfly crushed between books. Suddenly, the pressure relaxed and her body flew through the air like a feather, then hit the ground like a rock.

She got up and brushed the dust from her coat. Looking around, she was delighted to find she was in a place she had never seen before. It seemed that in the moment her body had flown through the air she'd been transported to another world. But her delight quickly faded, for she saw, only a few steps away, the rusty iron railing. The entrenched barb twisted in the wall of her stomach. She opened her mouth to eject it, but hot, dry air thrust in between her lips. A small tear congealed in the corner of her right eye, scratching like a grain of sand.

Looking up and through the iron bars, she saw the black building spattered with yellow blotches that spoiled its original colour. She knew almost certainly that there was a connection between her deep-seated desire to retch and this building, for the feeling always crept upon her whenever she remembered it and grew steadily the nearer she was to it, reaching its climax when she saw it face to face.

She paused in front of the iron gateway, looking around, reluctant to enter. If she delayed for a moment, who knew? Perhaps at that very moment a bomb would descend on the hated building; or someone might drop a lighted cigarette butt in the file store? or the worn-out pump in the head of department's chest would stutter and he would have a heart attack!

But the moment passed and nothing happened. She placed one foot in the gateway, leaving the other in the street. Who knew what might happen from moment to moment? Many things happen from one moment to another. Thousands die, thousands are born, volcanoes erupt, earthquakes bury cities. Many things in life happen from one moment to the next, more than people imagine, for people imagine only what they know, what they understand. Who knows what it means for a rocket to be fired from one moment to another? a rocket with a nuclear warhead? What might be buried if it fell from the sky? Do people know that the sky is jewelled with millions of stars bigger, much bigger, than the earth? That if one of these suspended jewels fell to the earth it would consume it completely? Or would this ugly building alone escape? Would the head of department remain suspended in space above his office chair, licking his fingertips and carefully turning over the attendance register? Such a thing was inconceivable. She smiled, saying to herself, yes of course, it's inconceivable. But her smile froze when she found that – flesh and blood and fully conscious – she had entered the courtyard of the Ministry.

She stopped, tall and slender, staring wildly, in panic, as if her feet had led her to a minefield. Then she sensed some sudden movement in the courtyard. A sleek, black car with a red interior swished across the courtyard as though through water; she was aware that like a huge whale it slid to a stop before the white marble stairs. On each side of these stairs stood a row of statues, each clad in a yellow uniform.

From where had these statues come in that brief moment? Maybe they had always been there and she'd never noticed? There were many things she didn't notice even though they were there. Had she, for example, ever noticed those marble stairs of peerless white?

Her eyes widened in amazement when one of the statues left its place and stepped towards the car. Not stepped in the real sense but twitched and shuddered like a robot, its upper half folded over its lower half as it stretched out a long, stiff arm and opened the car door . . .

She blinked to expel the grain of sand in the corner of her right eye, but instead it pressed deeper. Through bloodshot eyes, she strained to see what might emerge from the car. First she saw the pointed, black tip of a man's shoe, attached to a short, thin grey-clad leg, then a large, white, conical head with a small, smooth patch in the centre, reflecting the sunlight like a mirror;

8

square, grey shoulders emerged next, followed by the second, short, thin leg . . . This body, emerging limb by limb, reminded her of a birth she had seen when she was a child. The car still stood, its curved black roof silhouetted against the entrance to the white marble stairs.

She saw the body laboriously climb the stairs. On each step, it paused, as if to catch its breath, and jerked its neck back. The large head swayed as if it would fall, but it remained securely attached to the neck.

At times it seemed to her as if she were watching this body through a diminishing lens, seeing it as the Tom Thumb of her grandmother's stories. At other times when, as now, she was distracted, this body's reality overpowered her distraction, revealing it as the under-secretary at the biochemistry ministry where she was an employee.

The spacious lobby swallowed him, the car slid away, the statues relaxed and loosened. They walked with flexible legs to the wooden bench by the stairs and sat down. As she passed, they stared at her, blankly, mouths half-open and eyes half-closed. One stuffed a piece of bread into his mouth, another fetched a plate of brown beans from beneath the bench.

She crossed the open courtyard and went to the back of the black building, which was like the back of anything, dirtier, coarser, rougher. She paused before the small wooden door that was covered by a mess of sooty shapes including human finger and hand prints and the letters of fragmented words. She saw the word 'vot . . .' but dirt had erased the rest.

She walked down the dingy, narrow corridor and climbed the stairs like an automaton, her practised feet jumped over the missing step, her body avoided the iron bar that protruded from the banisters, she reached the fourth floor and turned right to cross the long passageway. She caught the stale smell of urine and turned her head away from the lavatory door; beside it was the door into her office.

She walked over to her desk and sat down. Opening the drawer she took a small cloth and wiped off the dust so that its black skin showed. The skin was torn in places revealing the

9

desk's white body beneath. She replaced the cloth, looked up and saw three other desks crowded side by side; three mummified heads jutted out above them . . .

The urine smell lingered in her nose but now, added to it, was another: that of a stale, unaired bedroom. She got up to open the window, but a coarse voice – more like the grunt of a sick animal – said: 'It's cold. Don't open it!'

She returned to her desk, took out a large file and examined the thick outer cover. On it in her own handwriting on a small, white label were the words 'Biochemical Research'. The letters were written with care and elegance, each etched in ink; she recalled how she had pressed the pen on each letter. The pen had been new, the inkpot too, and she could still remember the smell of the ink. Yes, though it was six years ago, she still remembered that smell and the curve of her fingers as she pressed out the letters. She had signed the acceptance for the new job in the biochemical research department and her fingers had trembled as she wrote her name on the official document, the first time she had put her name to an official document, the first time her signature had had an official value.

She opened the file's cover, revealing its yellow interior. Attached to its centre was a thin metal strip from which hung a white sheet of paper with not a single line on it. She closed the file and returned it to the drawer, then raised her head to the sky, but her eyes were stopped by the ceiling. She got up and went to the window to look at the sky through the dirty glass.

Something about the sky relaxed her, perhaps its unfathomable spaciousness, perhaps its deep, steady blue; or perhaps because the sky reminded her of Farid.

She didn't know what connected the sky and Farid but she knew there was a connection; maybe because the sky was always there when Farid was or because it was also there when he was absent? Farid had not come last night. It was the first time he had broken a date. He had not telephoned or apologized. What had happened?

The sky, silent and still, seemed as if in collusion with him.

The white clouds continued to drift, unconcerned, and the tree tops were lifted above the distant dark buildings.

Farid was absent for a reason. Everything in life happens for a reason. Things may seem to happen without reason, but sooner or later a reason becomes apparent. But what was the reason? Had there been an accident or an illness or the death of someone close? Or maybe something else? She drummed her fingers on the window-pane. Yes, maybe there was something else – something that Farid wanted to hide. He used to hide things, he hid papers in the drawer of his desk, and sometimes he would close the door when speaking on the telephone.

Such things were normal and unremarkable. Everyone has secrets. Old love letters, unpaid bills, rental contracts on plots of land in the country, a picture of one's mother in a *galabiyya* and wooden clogs, or of oneself as a child wearing a *tarbush* with the tassel missing. Yes, there were always things to hide in a drawer, things one did not always need. Putting them into a locked drawer at the bottom of the desk was blameless. But the long telephone conversations behind closed doors . . . how to explain them?

She ground the heel of her shoe into the floor and it stuck in a jagged hole in the wood. She tugged to get it out and her shoe came off. She bent down to release the heel, looking around, but the three bowed heads had moved only slightly. She looked at the clock. It was half past ten – three and a half hours before she could leave this graveyard. Sitting down at her desk for a moment, she looked again at the clock; the thin hands had stuck. Tucking her bag under her arm, she got up and strode out.

At the end of the corridor she paused momentarily before going down the stairs. She thought of going up to the fifth floor to apologise to the head of department for leaving early, and put a foot on the stairs. But, instead she descended quickly, shrugging her shoulders and burying her head in the wide collar of her coat.

She soon left the iron railing behind and reached the wide, crowded street, lifting her head from the concealing coat collar. The sun's rays on her back were pleasurable; the pleasure would have been greater except for the weight on her heart. She saw a woman sitting on the pavement, her empty hand outstretched, a young child in her lap. The sun bathed her whole body as she sat silent and still. She was not running away from the Ministry, neither was her heart heavy with such worries.

In the midst of the hurrying crowd, she glimpsed a tall, slender woman who resembled herself. She was walking quickly, pushing forward as if she were about to break into a run but was too embarrassed to do so. A bag swung from her hand, a black leather bag like those carried by doctors or lawyers or civil servants; no doubt it was full of important papers. Its owner waved down a taxi, leaped into it and vanished. She knew where she was going and her movements were light and energetic. Clearly, she was very busy, very engrossed, very absorbed. She had an important job and was happy with it, pleased with herself, felt herself to be important. Yes, that tall, slender young woman was important.

She closed her lips sternly, swallowing hard. Someone important like her would not be idly and aimlessly wandering the streets. She was envious; yes, envy was the word to describe her feelings at that moment. She was unsure of the meaning of the word 'envy' but had inherited it as she'd inherited her nose and arms and eyes. She knew that envy was an extrinsic act, that she couldn't envy herself, that there had to be another person to envy, a person who had to possess enviable characteristics, something important, not important in itself but important to her.

She put her hand into her coat pocket and played with the holes in the silky lining as if searching for something important within herself. Suddenly she discovered that there was nothing important about herself. But it was not exactly a discovery, neither was it sudden, but rather a slow, insidious, obscure feeling, which had started some time ago, perhaps after she'd graduated, perhaps after she'd begun working at the Ministry, perhaps only yesterday when she'd gone to the restaurant and found the table empty, or perhaps this morning when that

12

pointed thing had pushed between her legs as she jumped off the bus.

She swallowed bitter saliva and moved her dry tongue, saying to herself in an almost audible voice: 'Yes, I am nothing.' She would have repeated 'yes, I am nothing' but her lips tightened and instead the words died inside her mouth where they burned like acid.

She raised her head, her eyes roamed the sky as if in search of something. Yes, she was looking for something. She recalled her mother's voice saying: 'May the Lord make you successful, Fouada my daughter, and may you make a great discovery in chemistry.' She saw the blueness was pock-marked and white clouds drifted indifferently over it. She bowed her head and whispered: 'Your hopes are disappointed, mother, and your pleas are dashed against a silent sky.'

She bit her lip. A great discovery in chemistry! What did her mother know about chemistry? What did she know about any discoveries? Fouada was her only daughter, she laid all her failed ambitions on to her and, unlike other mothers these days, did not think about marriage. Her ambitions were not of the ordinary female type. Before getting married, she had gone to school and perhaps read some stories or a novel about an educated girl who had become great, perhaps the story of Madame Curie or some other memorable woman. But one morning, she had opened her eyes and had not found her school pinafore hanging up where she had left it the previous night, and heard her father's gruff voice saying: 'You're not going to school.' She had run crying to her mother and asked her why. The reason was marriage. That was enough for her to hate him from the first glance and she continued to hate him until he died. After his death, while Fouada was still in secondary school, her mother had said, combing her soft black hair in front of the mirror and looking at her slender figure:

'Your future lies in studying, my daugher. There's no use in men.'

Her mother hoped that Fouada would enter medical school, but her grade at the end of the secondary stage was too low.

13

Perhaps she hadn't studied enough or because in the history class she sat near the window and her eyes wandered to that tall tree laden with large red flowers, like a turban dusted with red copper powder. Sitting in the history lesson, she discovered she loved the colour of powdered red copper, that she loved chemistry and hated history. She could never remember the names of all the kings and rulers who had once governed Egypt, neither did she understand why the living should waste time on the deeds of the dead. Her father was dead and she had perhaps been a little happy when he died, although not for any particular reason; her father had been nothing particular in her life. He was simply a father, but she was happy, because she felt that her mother was happy. Some days later, she heard her say that he hadn't been much use. She was totally convinced of her words. Of what use had her father been.

She saw her father only on Fridays. Usually, he came home after she'd gone to sleep and left before she awoke and the house was quiet and clean, every day except Friday. Her father flooded the bathroom when he took a bath, soaked the living-room when he left the bathroom, threw his dirty clothes everywhere, raised his gruff voice from time to time, coughed and spat a lot, and blew his nose loudly. His handkerchief was very large and always filthy. Her mother put it in boiling water and said to her: 'That's to get rid of the germs.' At the time, Fouada did not know what 'germs' meant, but she heard the biology teacher say in one of the classes that germs were small, harmful things. That day, the teacher had asked the class: 'Where are these things to be found, girls?' The class was silent and none of the girls raised her hand, but Fouada raised hers confidently and proudly. The teacher smiled at her courage and said gently: 'Do you know where germs are found, Fouada?' Fouada got to her feet, head above the other girls, and said in a loud, confident voice, 'Yes, miss. Germs are found in my father's handkerchief.'

*   *   *

Fouada found herself at home, in her bedroom, sitting on the edge of the bed and staring at the telephone. She had no idea

14

how she had got there or how her legs had carried her on and off the bus at the right stops, how they had carried her from the bus stop to the house or how they had done all this of their own accord without her knowledge. But she gave this matter little thought as she did not suppose this to be a characteristic or distinction peculiar to her own legs. A donkey's legs did the same thing, quietly and silently.

She reached for the telephone, put a finger in the hole and dialled the familiar five numbers. She heard it ring, and leaned against the bedrest, preparing for a long reprimand. But the ringing went on. She looked at the clock. Midday. Farid did not leave the house before one or two. Was he reading in bed? There was a long passageway between the bedroom and the study where the telephone was. Was he in the bathroom and could not hear the phone from behind the closed door? She looked up to the window and saw a branch of the eucalyptus tree playing against the pane. Trees, too, could play. The receiver was still pressed to her ear, the bell was still ringing loudly. Something occurred to her and she put the receiver down for a moment, then, lifting it, redialled the number, carefully ensuring that her finger followed the correct sequence. Immediately the dial stopped after the five turns the ringing pierced her ear like a missile. She pressed the receiver to her ear for a long time; long enough for someone to come out of the bathroom or awaken from sleep. Another idea occurred to her and she replaced the receiver for a moment, then lifted it and called the operator. She asked, was there a fault on the line? A moment later, a gentle voice replied:

'The telephone is in order. It's ringing for you.'

The bell's brazen sound again filled her ear, sharp, loud and continuous. She hung up, leaned her head against the pillow and stared at the window.

Never before had she thought about her relationship with Farid; she had simply lived it. There was no room for both – either live it or think about it. Farid was always busy, spending hours with his books and papers, either writing or reading things, which he put away carefully in the drawer of his desk and locked

15

with a key. He went out every evening and stayed out late. Some nights he stayed away from home. She never asked him where he went, not wanting to take on the role of inquisitive wife, not wanting to take on the role of wife at all. She valued her freedom, her own room, her own bed, her own secrets, her own mistakes – they weren't really mistakes. Sometimes she loved to disappear and Farid did not know where she was. She delighted to hear words of admiration from a man's mouth, a delicious but never surprised delight, for she was sure something in her was worthy of admiration. But Farid was the centre of her life. Other days she swallowed like a dose of bitter medicine, then Tuesday would arrive in all its wondrous splendour. For on Tuesday she met Farid. Every Tuesday, at eight in the evening in that small restaurant when the weather was warm, or at his house on cold winter nights. How many winters had their relationship seen? She didn't know exactly, only that she had known Farid for a long, perhaps very long time.

How many winters had passed, how many Tuesdays! And every Tuesday, Farid had been waiting, had not lied once. If he concealed some things from her, he never lied, even when the question of marriage had somehow arisen. Looking at her with shining brown eyes, he had told her: 'I can never marry.' If any other man had said that to her, she might have doubted him or have felt it as an insult. But Farid was different, with him everything became different. Even words lost their familiar, traditional meaning and the names of things might suddenly become inapplicable, meaningless. The word 'dignity' for example. What does it mean? To preserve one's self-respect? Against whom? Against others? Yes. There must be others before whom one's self-respect must be protected.

But between her and Farid, there were no 'others', or any such thing as her self against his self. They shared everything in love, even their selves – she became him and he became her. He protected her rights and she his. Something strange, something extraordinary happened between them, but it happened effortlessly, spontaneously – as naturally as breathing.

Hearing her mother in the living-room shuffling towards her

door, she quickly got up from the bed and began moving around the room. She did not want her to come in and see her looking solemn and staring into space, like a sick person. Her mother stood at the door in her white headscarf and long *galabiyya*, saying in a hoarse, faint voice:

'I see you're wearing outdoor clothes. Are you going out?'

'Yes.'

'And lunch?' her mother said.

Fouada picked up her handbag, ready to leave, saying:

'I'm not hungry.'

Fouada didn't know why she was going out. Only that she didn't want to stay in, but to move, to see movement around her, to hear a loud clamour, louder than that bell that rang, persistently, endlessly in her ear. She left her street and turned right to walk alongside the stone wall to the flower garden. White jasmine glinted like silver in the bright sunlight. As usual, she reached out to pluck a spray, crushing it between her fingers and breathing in its scent. The heavy weight in her heart moved. The scent of jasmine was for her meeting Farid, his kiss on her neck. But now its poignant scent seemed to epitomize his absence, and confused feelings of nostalgia and reality stirred deep inside her. It was all like an illusion, like a dream, that ends when you awaken.

She let the crushed jasmine flowers fall from her fingers, and walked along the narrow street, turning into Nile Street. Suddenly she knew she hadn't left the house without reason or simply to move; she had a particular goal. A few more steps and she found herself in front of the small restaurant.

She hesitated, then entered, crossing the long passageway between the trees. Her heart began to pound, imagining that emerging from the passageway she would see Farid sitting at the white-cloth decked table, his back towards her, his face to the Nile, his shoulders tilted forward slightly, black hair falling thickly behind his small flushed ears, long slender fingers on the table playing with a scrap of paper or turning the pages of the notebook he always kept with him, or doing something but never staying still.

Yes, she would see him sitting like that. She would tiptoe up behind him, put her arms round his head and cover his eyes with her hands. He would laugh and grab her hands and kiss each finger one by one.

Her heart was thumping violently when she reached the end of the passageway. She turned to the left and looked towards the table. She felt a stab in her heart. The table was empty and naked, with no white cloth. She approached and touched it, as if looking for something Farid had forgotten, a piece of paper he had left for her, but her fingers met only the smooth wooden surface, the wind battering it from all sides, like the trunk of an old tree.

The waiter came over, smiling, but looked down when he saw the look on her face. She walked towards the passage but before turning into it, spun around to look again at the table. It was still empty. She ran towards the passageway and hurriedly left the restaurant.

She found herself in Doqi Street. Seeing a bus about to move off, she jumped on to it without knowing where it was going. She got one foot on the platform, the other hung in the air. Hands reached out to help her on and she managed to push her foot between the others on the step. Long, strong arms surrounded her to prevent her falling, then she found herself huddled with the other bodies inside the bus.

One of millions, one of those human bodies crowding the streets, the buses, the cars and the houses. Who was she? Fouada Khalil Salim, born in Upper Egypt, identity card number 3125098. What would happen to the world if she fell under the wheels of a bus? Nothing. Life would go on, indifferent and unconcerned. Maybe her mother would write her obituary in the paper, but what would a line in a newspaper do? What would it change in the world?

She looked around in surprise. But why surprise? She really was one of millions, really was one of the bodies crammed into the bus and if she fell under the wheels and died, her death would change nothing in the world. What was so astonishing

18

about that? But it still surprised her, amazed her, something that she could neither believe nor accept.

For she was not one of millions. Deep inside something assured her that she was not one of millions, was not simply a moving lump of flesh. She could not live and die without the world changing at all. Yes, in her heart of hearts something assured her, and not hers alone but in her mother's heart, and her chemistry teacher's – and in Farid's heart.

She heard her mother's voice saying: 'You will be someone great like Madame Curie', then the voice of her chemistry teacher saying: 'Fouada is different from the other girls in the class', and Farid's voice whispered in her ear: 'You have something in you that other women don't have.'

But what was the use of these voices, these words? They had resounded once or twice, vibrations disturbing the air, then they were over. Her mother had said it to her when she was young, a long time ago. The chemistry teacher had said it when she was in secondary school many years ago. And Farid, yes Farid too had told her, but Farid's voice had vanished into the air and he himself had disappeared as if he had never existed.

A fat woman stepped on her foot. The conductor tapped her shoulder to pay for the ticket. A large hand reached out from behind and pressed her thigh. Yes, one body amongst others crowding the world, filling the air with the smell of sweat, one of millions, millions, millions. Unaware, she said aloud: 'Millions, millions!' The fat woman stared at her with large, cow-like eyes and breathed a smell of onions into her face so that she turned away. Through the window she saw Tahrir Square and with all her strength pushed her way out of the bus.

*   *   *

She stood in the huge square, looking around and up at the tall buildings, their façades plastered with names written in broad lettering: doctors, lawyers, accountants, tailors and masseuses. She particularly noticed a sign on which was written: 'Abd al-Sami's Analysis Laboratory'. Suddenly, something dawned on her, as if a small searchlight had focused in her head. The idea

19

flashed through her mind as clear as a new light. It had always been there, hidden in the recesses, unmoving, but it was there and she knew it.

Now it had begun to move, to emerge from its hidden corner into the field of light. Fouada could read it, yes, written in clear broad letters on the façade of the building: 'Fouada's Chemical Analysis Laboratory'.

That was the deep-seated idea in her head. She didn't know when it had begun, for she merely remembered dates and was not good at calculating time. Time could pass quickly, very quickly, as quickly as the rotation of the earth. Sometimes it seemed to her that it did not move at all, and at others that it moved slowly, very slowly, and the earth trembled as though a volcano was erupting from its depths.

The idea had started long ago. It had occurred to her once when she was sitting in the chemistry class at school. It was not quite so clear but had appeared through a mist. She had been transfixed by a curious movement inside a test tube, colours that suddenly appeared and disappeared, vapours with strange smells, a different sediment at the bottom, a new substance – the result of the chemical interaction of two other substances – with new characteristics, new form, new wave-length. The chemistry lesson ended and she stayed in the laboratory, mixing substances together, observing the reactions with delight, sniffing the gas that rose from the mouth of the test tube, then shouting with joy: 'A new gas! Eureka!'

The slender, bullet-like body of the lab assistant rushed over and, exploding like flammable gas, yelled 'Get out!', snatching the test tube from her hands and pitching her discovery down the sink, cursing the day he had become a lab assistant in a wretched girls' school. He could have been an assistant in a college of science if he had completed his studies. She lost her temper when he threw her unique experiment down the drain and she cried: 'My discovery's lost!' She saw his look of contempt, then turned away and ran from the laboratory. His contemptuous glance haunted her and hindered her experimentation for a long time, and might have ultimately deterred her from pursuing the idea of discovery, but her mind was obsessed with the chemistry class and the chemistry teacher.

The chemistry teacher was as tall and slender as herself, her eyes always smiled and radiated a deeply thoughtful and confident look. It seemed to her that this look was directed towards her alone and not to the other girls in the class. Why? She didn't know exactly. There was no real proof of it, but she felt it, felt it forcefully, especially when she ran into her in the school yard, looked at her, then smiled. She didn't smile at all the girls. No, she didn't smile at everyone. That had been the historic day when the inspector had come and the teacher asked a question that nobody in the class – only Fouada – could answer. That day, she heard the teacher say, in front of the whole class and the inspector too: 'Fouada is different from the other girls.' That was exactly what she'd said, no more, no less. It was engraved in her brain just as she had pronounced it, word for word, with the same pauses, the same intonation, the same punctuation. The word 'different' was etched especially deeply, the first syllable emphasized . . .

Yes, Fouada loved chemistry. Not with an ordinary love like her love for geography, geometry and algebra, but something extraordinary. As she sat in the chemistry lesson, her brain would leap alertly and, like a magnet, everything around her was liable to stick to it – the teacher's voice, her words, her glances; particles of powdered substances might fly through the air, metallic fragments might scatter over the table, particles of vapour and gases might drift through the room. Every particle, every tremor, every vibration, every movement and every thing – her brain picked them all up, just as magnets attract and hold metal particles.

After all this, it was inevitable that her mind turned to chemistry and for everything around her to take on chemical forms and qualities. It was not unusual for her to feel one day that the history teacher was made of red copper, that the drawing teacher was made of chalk, that the headmistress was made of manganese, that hydrogen sulphide gas came out of the mouth of the Arabic teacher, that the sound of the hygiene teacher's voice was like the rattle of tin fragments.

All the teachers, men and women, acquired mineral qualities, except one – the chemistry teacher. Her voice, eyes, hair, shoulders, arms and legs, everything about her was utterly human, was alive, moved and pulsated like arteries of the heart. She was a living person of flesh and blood with absolutely no relation to minerals.

But her voice was the most remarkable thing about her. It had a fragrance as sweet as orange blossom or a small, untouched jasmine flower. Fouada would sit in the chemistry class, her eyes, ears, nose and pores open to the sweet voice, the words seeping in through all these openings like pure, warm air.

One day, the voice brought her the story of the discovery of radium. Previously, it had brought her the names of famous men who had discovered things. She would bite her nails as she listened, telling herself that if she were a man she would be able to do likewise. Obscurely, she felt that these discoverers had no greater talent for discovery than she, only that they were men. Yes, a man could do things a woman could not simply because he was a man. He was not more able, but he was male, and masculinity in itself was one of the preconditions for discovery.

But here was a woman who had made a discovery, a woman like her, not a man. The obscure feelings about her ability to make a discovery became clearer and she grew more convinced that there was something that waited for her to lift a veil and discover it, something that existed, like sound and light and gases and vapours and uranium rays. Yes, something existed that only she knew about.

*　　*　　*

Fouada found her body stretched out on her bed with her eyes fixed on the ceiling, on a small, jagged patch where the white paint had flaked off to reveal the cement beneath. Her feet were sore from so much walking around the streets off Tahrir Square. She didn't really know why she had walked, but it was as if she were searching for something. Perhaps she was searching for

Farid amongst the people she encountered, because she stared into men's faces and examined the heads of people who passed by in cars or taxis; or perhaps it was an empty apartment she was looking for, because here and there she would pause in front of a new building and stare confusedly at the caretaker.

But now she was staring at a jagged patch of ceiling, not thinking of anything in particular. Hearing the sound of her mother shuffling towards her room, she quickly pulled up the cover and closed her eyes, pretending to be asleep. She heard her mother's panting breath and knew that she was standing at the doorway watching her sleep. Fouada tried to keep still and to let her chest rise and fall with regular, deep breathing. Then her mother's footstep shuffled away from her room. She might have opened her eyes and resumed staring at the ceiling, but she felt relaxed with her eyes closed and thought she might sleep. But then she leaped out of bed, for an idea had struck her. She wrapped herself in a large overcoat and made for the door of her room but then hesitated, walked to the telephone and dialled the five numbers. The ringing was sharp, shrill and uninterrupted. Replacing the receiver, she hurriedly left the house.

She walked rapidly, her feet taking her from street to street. She jumped on to a bus whose number she recognized, got off at a stop she knew only too well and turned right into a small street, knowing that at the end of it was a white three-storey house with a small wooden door.

The dark-skinned caretaker was sitting on his bench at the entrance to the stairs. She was just about to ask after Farid when she caught that inquisitive glance common to all caretakers. He knew her, had seen her time and again going up to Farid's apartment, but each and every time he gave her the same searching look, as if not recognizing the relationship that existed between herself and Farid. She bounded up the stairs, then stood panting in front of the dark-brown, wooden door. The kitchen window overlooking the stairs was open. So Farid was in, hadn't had an accident as she had imagined, hadn't been carried away by the sky. Her heart beat painfully and she considered leaving quickly before he saw her. He had missed their date on purpose, not by accident, and had not telephoned her to explain why. She would have turned on her heel and left except that she saw no light behind the glass peep-window. The apartment was in total darkness. Maybe he was reading in his bedroom and the bedroom light did not reach that far?

She pressed the bell and heard the high-pitched ringing in the flat. She kept her finger on the bell and the sound rang loud and hard in the living-room but no one came to the door. She took her finger off the bell and the sound stopped. Again, she pressed it and again the loud, harsh sound reverberated through the living room in the apartment without anyone opening the door. She put her ear to the door hoping to hear the sound of movement or stifled breathing or a sigh, but nothing. Then suddenly, the sound of the telephone ringing came from the study and she leaped backward, imagining that it was herself calling him from her house. But she was standing in front of the door so it couldn't be her phoning him now. The telephone continued to ring for a few moments, then stopped. Her ear to the door, she heard nothing to indicate the presence of a living being in the apartment. Hearing the clatter of stiletto heels coming up the stairs, she moved away from the door a little and pressed the bell again. From the corner of her eye, she saw a fat woman climbing the stairs. She kept pressing the bell, looking ahead until the woman vanished around the bend of the staircase. She waited a few minutes more until the sound of the thin, clattering heels stopped, and then slowly and heavily made her way downstairs.

She let her feet take her where they would. Thoughts raced through her head almost audibly. Farid had failed to meet her on Tuesday, had not telephoned her and was not at home. Where could he be? He could not be in Cairo or in a nearby town. He must be somewhere far away, where there was no phone or post office. Why was he hiding the reason for his absence from her? Didn't their relationship make it his duty to say? But what sort of relationship was it that made it a person's duty to act in a particular way towards another person? What was it that made it his duty? Love?

The word weighed in her mouth like a stone. Love. What

24

did love mean? When had she first heard it? From whose mouth? She did not remember precisely, but the word had been in her ear all her life. She used to hear it often and because she heard it often, she did not know it, like the feminine parts of herself which she often saw attached to her body and washed with soap and water every day without knowing them. Her mother was the cause. Perhaps if she'd been born without a mother, she would have known everything spontaneously. When she was very young, she learned that she had been born from an opening beneath her mother's stomach, perhaps the same opening through which she urinated or another one nearby. But when she told her mother of her discovery, she scolded her and said that she'd been born from her ear. With this explanation, her mother perverted her natural feelings and many of her intuitions were blocked for a long while. For a time, she tried to create a relationship between hearing and birth, sometimes doubting that the ear was for hearing but rather, perhaps, that it was made for married women to urinate from. She did not understand why she always linked birth to urinating and felt that the two must be related. She continued searching for the site of the opening through which she had emerged into the world and thought she might find out in the history or geography or hygiene class, but they taught her everything but that. She had a lesson on chickens and how they laid and hatched eggs, a lesson on fish and how they reproduced, a lesson on crocodiles and snakes and every living creature except humans. They even studied how date-palms pollinated each other. Could the date-palm be more important to them than themselves? Towards the end of the year, she put up her hand and asked the hygiene teacher; but she considered the question to be rude and punished her by making her stand against the wall with her arms up. Staring at the wall, Fouada wondered why plants, insects and animals impregnated each other and this was considered one of the sciences, whereas in the case of humans, it was considered something shameful that merited punishment?

*   *   *

25

Fouada found she was walking along Nile Street. Heavy darkness covered the surface of the water, the lights of circular lamps reflected on both sides. As it slid along in the darkness, the long and slender Nile looked like the flirtatious body of a woman in black, mourning for a hated husband, beads of imitation pearls dotting the sides of her black gown. Looking around her in the dark, everything seemed dream-like, surreal. Even the door of the small restaurant overhung with cheap coloured lights projected an eerie, ghostly shadow. She passed by the door without going in, but then retraced her steps and entered. She walked down the path under the trees and at the end turned to look at the table. It was not empty. A man and a woman were sitting there. The waiter was laying glasses and plates in front of them, giving them the same smile that he gave herself and Farid. She turned quickly before he saw her, and left the restaurant.

She walked down Nile Street, head lowered. What had brought her here? Didn't she know that these places were in collusion with Farid, declared his absence and hid him? Hypocrisy and contradiction engulfed her like a dark web. She stamped her foot in anger. What had got into her? Farid had left her and vanished, so why was she hovering around his places? Why? She must banish him from her life just as he had banished her from his. Yes, she must.

The very thought seemed to calm her and she looked up at the street. But her heart lurched violently for she had seen a man coming towards her who walked like Farid. She hurried towards him. His shoulders were hunched slightly and he moved slowly and cautiously. The same movements as Farid! They came closer and closer. He swung his arms in a particular way, not like Farid did. When he was a few steps away, she opened her mouth to gasp: Farid! but the light of a passing car swept the shadow from a face that was not his. Her heart fell like a lump of lead and she shrank into her coat. The man nodded his bald head suggestively. She turned away and hurried off, but he walked behind her, whispering half-formed, incomprehensible words. She turned off Nile Street into a side road and he followed, continuing to stalk

26

her from street to street until she reached the front of her own house.

*   *   *

She opened the door panting. Not hearing her mother's voice, she tiptoed across the living-room to see her mother through the open door of her room asleep in bed. She was lying on her right side, her head wrapped in a white shawl and raised on two thick pillows, her thin body hidden under a folded woollen blanket.

Fouada went into her room and closed the door. She stood motionless in the centre for a while, then began to get undressed. She put on a nightdress, took off her watch and put it on the shelf beside the telephone. As her hand touched the cold telephone, she shivered and looked at the time. It was midnight. Was Farid at home? Should she try and call him? Shouldn't she stop this pursuit? She could always dial the number and, if he answered, she could hang up. Yes, he would not know who was calling.

She put her finger in the dial and turned it five times. The familiar ringing sounded even louder in the quiet of the night. She covered the mouthpiece with the palm of her hand, thinking that the loud ring might awaken her mother. The bell continued to screech in her ear like a hungry animal, its echo pounding in her head and bouncing off it as though it were a wall of solid stone.

She replaced the receiver to stifle the screeching, threw herself on the bed and closed her eyes to sleep. But she did not sleep. Her body remained outstretched on the bed, her head on the pillow. She opened her eyes and saw the wardrobe, the mirror, the clothes-stand, the shelf, the window and the white ceiling with the jagged patch from which the paint had fallen. She closed her eyes and let her chest rise and fall with deep, regular breathing. But still she did not sleep. Her body remained, with all its weight and density, on the bed. She turned on to her stomach, burying her face in the pillow, pretending to lose consciousness. But she remained conscious, her body stretched out under the coarse woollen cover. She rolled over on to her left

27

side and opened her eyes, seeing nothing except the darkness. She imagined that her eyes were still closed or that she had lost her sight, but a faint strip of light presently appeared on the wall. She pressed her head into the pillow and pulled the cover over her eyes, but still could not sleep. The familiar weight of her head remained on the pillow. A soft hum began, very softly at first, then it gradually grew louder until it became a sharp continuous whistle like the ringing of an unanswered bell. She imagined that the telephone receiver was by her ear and put her hand under her head, but found only the pillow. The humming stopped when she took her ear off the pillow, then began again. She held her breath for a moment and the source of the sound became clear. It was those familiar repeated beats of her heart, but on no previous night had they been as strongly audible as a hammer nor so continuous. On any other night, she put her head down on the pillow without hearing anything and in a few moments was fast asleep. How did she used to fall asleep? She tried to find out how she slept every night, but suddenly discovered that she did not know. Her body felt heavy, as if shackled with chains, and then she lost consciousness. She remembered that once or twice she had tried to find out how she lost consciousness in sleep and had opened her eyes before drifting off, hanging on to the very last moment of consciousness to see what was happening to her, but sleep always overcame her before she found out.

Really, she knew nothing, not even the simplest things. She did not know by intuition and did not learn from repetition. How many nights of her life had she slept away? She was now aged thirty, every year had three hundred and sixty five days, so she had slept ten thousand, nine hundred and fifty nights without knowing why.

She pressed her head into the pillow. The humming echoed in her head, a head as solid as stone, a head that knew nothing, did not know where Farid had vanished, did not know why she had gone to the college of science, did not know why she was working in the biochemical research department of the Ministry, did not know what chemical research to do, did not know the old, deep-seated discovery which had to be found, did not know how to sleep. Yes, an ignorant solid head of stone that knew nothing and was only able to repeat this empty echo, like a wall.

It seemed to her that a heavy, high wall had fallen on her and that her body was being crushed into the ground. She felt water surround her from all sides as if she were swimming in a deep and wide sea. Although she didn't know how to swim, she swam with the utmost skill as if flying through the air. The water was deliciously warm. She saw a huge shark glide under the water, its great jaws open, in each jaw long, pointed teeth. The beast came nearer and nearer, its mouth opening into a long dark tunnel. She tried to get away but couldn't. She screamed in terror and opened her eyes.

*   *   *

Daylight was filtering through the narrow slats of the shutters. She lifted her head from the pillow and, feeling dizzy, put it down again. Then she reached out and took the watch off the shelf. Glancing at it, she jumped out of bed and dressed quickly. She gulped down the cold cup of tea her mother had prepared and went out into the street.

The cold air struck her face and she shivered and moved her arms and legs briskly, but suddenly felt a pain in her stomach and slowed down. She pressed her fingers to the soft triangle beneath her ribs and located the pain, deep inside her flesh, gnawing at the wall of her stomach like a worm with teeth. She didn't know the reason for this strange pain which attacked her every morning.

She waited at the bus stop, but when the 613 to the Ministry came, she stood still and stared at it. As it moved off, she realized that she ought to be on it and ran after it, but couldn't catch it. She went back to the stop, feeling a sense of relief. She would not go to the Ministry today. All her leave had been used, but what would happen if she didn't go today . . . would it change anything in the world? Not even her death or flesh and blood absence from the world would change anything, so how important would be her absence from the Ministry today? One blank space in the old attendance register with its tattered cover.

The world around her brightened at the thought. She looked at the people contemptuously as they ran panting for the buses, blindly hurling themselves on to them. Why were these fools running? Did any one of them know how they slept last night? Did any one of them know that if they fell under the wheels and died or if the whole bus overturned with them and everyone inside and was submerged in the Nile, did they know that this would mean nothing to the world?

Another bus stopped in front of her. There were some empty seats, so she got on and sat down beside an old man. He was holding yellow prayer beads between his trembling fingers, softly muttering: 'Oh Protector! Oh Protector! Lord protect us! Lord protect us!' from time to time peering from the windows up at the sky through encrusted, lashless eyes. It seemed to Fouada that some catastrophe had just that minute befallen the man so she smiled at him gently to console him, but he took fright and cowered into his seat away from her, his thin body pressing up against the window. 'How much fear there is in the world!' she said to herself and turned away.

On the other side, a young woman stood beside her. The bus was now packed with standing passengers. A waft of perfume came from the woman, on her face that familiar layer of powder, on her lips that blood-red coating. Her body was slim and so short that her stomach bumped against Fouada's shoulder as she sat, but her buttocks were round and prominent behind her.

For no reason, Fouada suddenly jumped up. The woman squeezed into the seat in her place, huffing in irritation. Fouada pushed her way through the bodies, then hurled herself from the bus before it pulled away from the stop, her feet landing on the ground. She almost fell over but managed to stay upright and, looking up to see where she was, found herself in front of the rust-covered railings of the Ministry.

Like a bucketful of cold water in her face she realized where she was, remembering that she had intended not to go to the Ministry. But unknowingly her feet had brought her along the

30

usual daily path, like a donkey before whom the door of the barn opens and who emerges alone and automatically into the field. And since it is automatic, it is very natural, like a baby emerging from its mother's womb.

She looked up at the gloomy building and saw it bulging out of the open courtyard, like her mother's stomach. Long wide cracks spread over its dark brown surface like stretch marks. She caught a strange smell, like the one she smelled in hospital maternity wards or in stale toilets. As she stumbled forward, the feeling of nausea intensified and she knew she was approaching her office.

*   *   *

The head of department was angry. He spoke loudly, saliva sprayed from his lips and a drop landed on her cheek. She left it there and did not wipe it off with her handkerchief, pretending to be unaware of it.

'You left your office before time yesterday, three and a half hours early!' she heard him say.

The word 'yesterday' resonated in her ear and without thinking she repeated:

'Yesterday?'

The director's thick lips curled in disdain and his shiny bald head nodded as he shouted:

'Yes, yesterday, or have you forgotten?'

As if talking to herself, she said:

'No, I haven't forgotten, but I thought that it happened . . .' She swallowed the rest of the sentence '. . . a week or two ago.'

He continued speaking loudly, but she was not listening. She was wondering about the way people spend their time, how feelings of time do not always correspond to the number of hours or minutes that pass. Can the steady and continuous movement of the hands of a clock inside that limited, small circle be an accurate measure of time? How is it possible to measure something invisible and unlimited by something visible and limited? How do we measure something we don't see or feel or touch or

31

taste or smell or hear? How do we measure something non-existent with something existent?

A thought occurred to her which she believed no one else had ever had. She felt a secret joy, the signs of which she hid from the head of department. She didn't know why or how she opened her mouth but suddenly she said to him:

'I've been working in this research department for six years now, and I believe I have the right to carry out research from today.'

As if she had delivered an insult, the director's bald head turned red and, sitting at his desk, he looked like an ape standing on its head, its behind in the air.

'Why are you smiling like that?'

She tightened her lips so as not to answer him, but instead blurted out:

'You may have the right to dock me for the time I was absent, but you have no right to ask me why I am smiling!'

She imagined that he would get even angrier and his voice get even louder, but he suddenly fell silent as if stunned by her unusual ability to answer back. His silence encouraged her to pretend to be angry and, raising her voice, she said:

'I do not accept that anyone, no matter who, should trample on my rights, and I know how to defend them!'

The redness of his bald head faded to a pale yellow, making it look like a melon.

'What rights of yours have I trampled on?' he exclaimed in astonishment.

Waving a hand in the air, she shouted:

'You trampled on two important rights . . . first when you asked me why I was smiling, and second when you finished the question with the words 'like that'. The first right is my right to smile, and the second right is my absolute right to choose how I smile.'

His deep-set eyes widened, creasing the cushions of flesh around them, and he gasped in utter amazement:

'What is it you're saying, miss?'

Fouada was shaken by an inexplicable anger and without thinking snapped:

'And who told you I was a miss?'

His eyes widened still further.

'Well, aren't you?' he said.

Fouada thumped the desk with her fist and shouted:

'How dare you ask me such a question. What gives you the right? The regulations . . . ?'

How had the scene changed so fast, so that now she, Fouada, was the angry one and had appropriated the right to be so? The head of department was now more afraid of her than surprised, and that fierce look with which he fixed his subordinates had vanished from his eyes to be replaced by a tame, almost respectful one, much like the one he gave the under-secretary and his immediate superiors. She heard him say in what would have been a gentle voice, had he practised the words over a number of years:

'It seems you're tired today. You're not yourself. I apologize if something I said offended you.'

He put his papers under his arm and left the room. She stared at his back as he went through the door. It was bent like an old man's, but not bent with age, rather with that premature curvature that afflicts civil servants from so much bowing and bending.

Leaving the Ministry that day, immediately she had left the rusty iron railings behind, Fouada told herself: 'I will never go back to that dingy tomb.' She didn't pay much heed to the phrase for she had said it every day for the last six years. She set off for the bus stop to make her way home, but when she reached it her feet carried on walking down the street. She didn't know where she was going, just went on, aimlessly. She looked at the people striding quickly, purposefully and with determination towards a definite and conscious goal. She wondered at how they could achieve such a miracle, and at the utter ease with which they moved their legs. She spun around not knowing which direction to take and experienced herself as alone, inside a closed circle. No one turned with her, no one was with her, no one at all.

33

She raised her head and, with a start, saw the tall buildings with placards fixed to the walls. She suddenly remembered that she had come to a decision sitting at her desk that morning, a final, an irreversible decision. Yes, she would rent a small apartment and turn it into her own chemical laboratory. She drew herself up and stamped her foot forcefully. Yes, that was her decision and that was her intention, and neither of them would she relinquish.

Finding herself in Qasr al-Nil Street she strolled along it examining the buildings. From time to time, she stopped to ask a caretaker if there was a vacant apartment. At the Opera end of the street, she crossed over and retraced her steps, scrutinizing the buildings on the other side.

One caretaker she asked peered at her with his dark face and bloodshot eyes, then asked:

'Have you got a thousand pounds with you?'

'What for?' she said.

'There's an apartment going vacant at the beginning of the month, but the owner wants to sell the furniture to whoever rents it.'

'Is the furniture in the apartment?' she asked.

'Yes,' he replied.

'Can I see it?'

'Yes,' he said.

She followed him into the lobby of the building. He went to the lift, pressed number 12 with a finger, long and thin, like a black pencil with a white tip. Going up, she asked:

'How many rooms are there in the apartment?'

'Two,' he replied.

'And the rent?'

'It used to be six pounds a month.'

'Who's the owner?'

'An important business man,' he answered.

'Does he live in it?' she inquired.

'No, it used to be his office.'

The lift stopped on the twelfth floor. The caretaker went towards a large brown door bearing a small brass plate with the

34

number 129 on it. Opening the door he went in, she following behind, into a small living-room with a wide sofa whose seat sagged almost to the floor, two big, old chairs and a shabby wooden table. In the first room she saw a broad, blue, iron bed, a large chair and a clothes stand. Entering the other room, she thought there might be a desk, but saw another bed, a wardrobe and a mirror. Turning to the caretaker, she asked:

'Where's the desk?'

His bluish lips curled back to show their moist red underside and he said gruffly:

'Don't know. I'm only the caretaker.'

Fouada wandered through the apartment and went to the window. From its towering height, the apartment overlooked the heart of Cairo. She could make out the main streets and the squares, the bridges and forks of the Nile. Fouada had never been up so high and Cairo seemed to her smaller than she had thought. The crowd that used to swallow her up, the buses that could crush her, the network of long, wide streets in which she could get lost – all now were remote, unreal – no longer a great city, but an anthill, crawling and scurrying without purpose, without significance.

She was strangely delighted by this diminution of everything while she remained the same size and weight, standing by the window; perhaps was even larger and heavier compared to what she could see below?

She was aroused by the voice of the caretaker saying:

'Do you like the apartment, lady?'

She turned to him and dreamily replied:

'Yes.'

Glancing at the iron bed, she said:

'But can't the deposit be reduced? This furniture isn't worth more than . . .'

The caretaker whispered in her ear:

'It's not worth anything, but these days the apartment . . . this apartment won't go for less than thirty or forty pounds a month.'

'That's true,' she said, 'but even if I put myself on the market I couldn't find a thousand pounds.'

The dark face smiled, revealing surprisingly white teeth.

'You're worth your weight in gold!' he said.

This flattery pleased Fouada hugely in a way she hadn't felt for a long time and she smiled broadly saying:

'Thank you, uncle . . .'

'Othman,' the caretaker said.

'Thank you, Uncle Othman.'

They went back down in the lift. She shook the caretaker's hand, thanked him and was about to leave when he said:

'What do you want to rent an apartment for, lady? To live in?'

'No,' replied Fouada, 'it will be a chemistry laboratory.'

'Chemistry?' he exclaimed.

'Yes, chemistry.'

Again he smiled broadly and, as if he now understood, said:

'Ah, yes, yes, chemistry. A good apartment for it.'

'It's very good,' Fouada said 'but . . .'

The caretaker brought his lips close to her ear.

'You can come to an understanding with the owner. He might lower it to six hundred. You're the first one I've told this to, but you're a good person and deserve the best.'

'Six hundred?' Fouada said to herself. Could her mother give her six hundred? Uncertain, she looked at the caretaker.

'I can fix you an appointment with the owner if you like,' he said.

She opened her mouth to refuse, but instead said:

'Okay.'

'Tomorrow's Friday. He comes here every Friday to check the building.'

Smiling proudly, he added:

'He owns the whole building.'

'When will he be here? What time?' she asked.

'About ten in the morning,' he replied.

'I'll come at half past ten, but you must tell him that I don't have six hundred at the moment.'

'Pay what you have and the rest in instalments,' said the caretaker. 'I can fix it for you, he won't be too hard.'

With his mouth close to her ear again, he whispered:

'The apartment's been empty for seven months but you mustn't say you know this or he'll know that it was me who told you. You're the first one I've told this to, but you're a good person and deserve the best.'

Fouada smiled and said:

'Thank you, Uncle Othman. I'll repay you for this favour.'

His answering smile was full of expectation.

* * *

Fouada arrived home before dark. Her mother was sitting in the living-room wrapped in wool blankets. Om Ali, the cook, was with her. As soon as she heard Fouada enter, Om Ali got up, exclaiming:

'Thank goodness you've come.'

She enveloped her shrivelled body in a black wrap and tucked her small purse under her arm in readiness to go home. Fouada saw her mother's large eyes, a transparent shroud of pale yellow discoloured the whites. The tip of her nose was red as if she had caught a cold. She heard her say weakly:

'I've been worrying about you all day. Why didn't you phone?'

Sitting down at the table, Fouada said:

'There wasn't a phone nearby, mama.'

'Why? Where have you been all this time?' her mother asked.

Putting a spoonful of rice with tomato sauce into her mouth, she said:

'I was wandering the streets.'

Astonished, her mother exclaimed:

'Wandering the streets? Why?'

Swallowing her food she said:

'I was searching for a great discovery.'

Surprise creased her mother's face:

'What did you say?'

Fouada smiled, chewing a piece of grilled meat:

'Have you already forgotten your old prayer?'

And hunching her shoulders in imitation of her mother

37

preparing to make a supplication and in her accent Fouada proclaimed:

'May the Lord help you, Fouada my daughter, to make a great discovery in chemistry!'

Her mother's parched lips parted in a feeble smile and she said:

'How much I want that for you, my daughter.'

Feeling happy, Fouada selected a slice of tomato sprinkled with green pepper and said:

'It seems that your prayer may be answered.'

Her mother's happy beam etched her wrinkles deeper:

'Why? Have they given you a rise in the Ministry? Or a promotion?'

The Ministry! Why did she have to mention it? Couldn't she at least have waited until she'd finished eating? Fouada felt the pleasure of eating disappear and that chronic pain began to creep into her stomach accompanied by a dry nausea that would not move. Without replying, she got up to wash her hands but again heard her mother say:

'Make me happy, daughter. Have you been promoted?'

Fouada returned from the bathroom and stood in front of her mother.

'What's the use of a rise or promotion, mama?' she said. 'What's the use of the whole Ministry? You imagine the Ministry's something great, but it's only an old building on the verge of collapse. You imagine that when I leave here early every morning and come back every afternoon I've done some work at the Ministry, but you won't believe it if I tell you that I haven't done a thing, nothing at all, except write my name in the attendance register!'

Her mother stared at her with wide, jaundiced eyes and said sadly:

'But why don't you do anything? They won't be pleased with you for that and you won't get promoted.'

Fouada swallowed hard and said:

'Promotion! Promotion is given according to your birth certificate, according to the flexibility of your back!'

'The flexibility of your back?' her mother said in surprise. 'Are you in chemical research or in the sports department?'

Fouada laughed briefly, then put her fingers on her mother's mouth and said:

'Don't say research, it's a sensitive word!'

'Why?' her mother asked.

'Nothing, I was just teasing. What I mean is that I'm going to set up a chemistry laboratory.'

Fouada sat down beside her mother and eagerly explained what it would mean for her to have her own laboratory. She would carry out analyses for people and make a lot of money. Apart from this, she would do chemical research there and might discover something important to change the world. After this enthusiastic introduction, Fouada had to broach the tedious matter of finance, of asking her mother for money. Her mother had been listening closely and happily to everything Fouada was saying until the hints of requests for money. She understood that unmistakable tone in Fouada's voice that ultimately meant she was asking for something.

Finally, she said:

'That's very nice. All I can do is wish you every success, daughter.'

'But wishes alone aren't enough, mama,' Fouada said. 'I can't open a laboratory on wishes. I need money to buy materials and equipment.'

Waving her veined hands, her mother said:

'Money? And where should the money come from? You know the well's run dry.'

'But you once said you had about a thousand pounds.'

All weakness vanished from her mother's voice as she replied:

'A thousand? There's no longer a thousand. Have you forgotten we took some of it to whitewash the apartment and to modernize the furniture? Have you forgotten?'

'Did you spend the whole thousand?' Fouada asked.

Tightening her lips, her mother said:

'All that's left is enough for my funeral.'

'Perish the thought, mama' said Fouada.

39

In a frail voice and sighing feebly, her mother said:

'It's not far away, daughter. Who knows what can happen tomorrow. I had a bad dream a few days ago.'

'No ... no ... don't say such things,' exclaimed Fouada getting to her feet. 'You'll live to be a hundred. You're only sixty-five now, so you've still got thirty-five years of life ahead of you. And not just an ordinary life, but a happy and easy one because your daughter Fouada will achieve miracles in these years and money will rain down on you from the sky!'

Swallowing hard, her mother said:

'Why don't you save some money? I saved a thousand pounds from your father's pension which is three pounds less than your wages. Where does all your money disappear?'

'My money?' retorted Fouada. 'My wages aren't even enough to buy one good dress!'

There was a long moment of silence. Fouada walked to the door of her room and stood at the doorway for a while looking at her mother swathed in woollen covers on the sofa. A funeral or a great discovery? Which of the two was more important or useful? She opened her mouth to make a final attempt.

'So you won't give me anything?'

Without looking up, her mother replied:

'Do you want me to be buried without a coffin?'

Fouada went into her room and threw herself on to the bed. There was no hope left, nothing left, everything had vanished, everything was lost. The chemistry laboratory, research, Farid, the chemistry discovery. Nothing remained, nothing except her heavy, dejected body that ate and drank and urinated and slept and perspired. Of what use was it? Why was it the only thing that remained? Why it alone? Within that closed circle?

She stared at the white wall beside the wardrobe. There was something black on it, a square shape, a picture frame. It held the photograph of a girl in a long, white, bridal gown, holding a bouquet of flowers in her closed fingers, beside her a boy with a long face and black moustache. All her life, Fouada had seen this picture hanging in the living-room but had never stood in front of it and examined it. Her mother had told her it was her wedding picture but she had only glanced at it from afar as if it were some girl other than her mother.

Only once had Fouada happened to stand in front of the picture and study it. That was a year or so after her father died. Her history teacher had hit her over the hands twenty times with a ruler, twice on each finger. Fouada had gone home and complained to her mother and she had slapped her face for neglecting history. Then she went to the dressmaker's, leaving Fouada alone in the house. She didn't know why she had stood in front of the picture that day, but she wandered about the house, staring at the walls as though in prison. For the first time she saw the picture. For the first time she saw her father's face. She studied his eyes for a long time and imagined that they resembled her own. And like a knife in her heart, she suddenly realized that she loved her father, that she wanted him, wanted him to look at her with those eyes and to hold her in his arms. She had buried her head in the pillow on the sofa and wept. She cried because when her father had died she hadn't cried, hadn't grieved. At that moment, she wished her father were alive so he could die again, so that she could cry to put her conscience to rest. She dried her eyes on the sofa cover, got up, took the picture off the hook, wiped the dust off the glass, and looked at it again. It was as if the dust had veiled her mother's eyes from her because they now appeared clear and wide and held a strange look she had never seen before, an ill-tempered, tyrannical look. Fouada lifted the picture to hang it back on the hook but then took it into her room, hammered in a nail beside the wardrobe and hung it up. Then she forgot about it and hardly looked at it again.

Now Fouada closed her eyes to sleep, but felt something under her eyelids, something like tears, but burning. She rubbed her eyes, wiped them with the corner of the bed cover, laid her head on the pillow and pulled up the bedclothes to sleep. But the buzzing began in her ears, like the faint, endless ringing of a bell. Remembering something, she jumped out of bed and dialled the five numbers on the telephone. The bell rang, loud and clear. The third night and Farid was not at home. Where could he be?

41

At one of his relatives'? But she didn't know any of his relatives. At one of his friends'? She didn't know any of his friends. She knew only him. She didn't know him in that traditional way, didn't know what his father did nor how many acres he might inherit from him nor how much he earned each month nor his position at work nor details like tax statements and deductions and passport number and date of birth. She knew nothing like that, but did know him in flesh and blood – the shape of his eyes and that unique thing that appeared in them, something with a life of its own. She knew the shape of his fingers, the way his lips parted in a smile, could distinguish his voice from all others, his walk from amongst hundreds, knew the taste of his kiss in her mouth, the touch of his hand on her body and his smell. Yes, she knew, could isolate that unusual and particular warm smell that preceded him just before he arrived and stayed with her after he left, that remained on her clothes, hair and fingers, as if it were another person inseparable from her or as if it emanated from her and not from him.

But was this all the information she had about Farid? The shape of his fingers, the movement of his lips, the way he walked and his smell? Could she walk around searching for him every-where, sniffing the air like a bloodhound? Why didn't she know more about him? Why didn't she know what his job was or where he worked? Why didn't she know where his family or relatives or friends lived? But he had never told her and she had never asked. Why should she? He didn't ask her. They had been colleagues in the college of science. That was how it had all begun.

Hearing a sound nearby Fouada opened her eyes and saw her mother standing beside the bed. Her eyes seemed even wider and more jaundiced and her face more lined. She heard her say:

'How much do you need to set up a laboratory?'

Fouada swallowed hard and said:

'How much do you have left?'

'Eight hundred pounds,' her mother replied.

'How much can you give me?'

The mother was silent for a moment, then said:

'One hundred.'

'I need two hundred,' Fouada said. 'I'll pay it back.'

She got out of bed saying:

'I promise I'll pay it all back to you.'

Her voice sad, the mother said:

'When? You haven't repaid your old debt.'

Fouada smiled and said:

'How can I repay it? You're asking me to repay you nine months' pregnancy, labour pains, the breast milk you fed me and nights awake beside the cradle! Can I ever repay you all that?'

'God will repay me for it, but you must return the hundred pounds you took last year.'

'Last year?' Fouada said distractedly.

'Have you forgotten?' her mother asked.

Fouada remembered that day a year ago. She had been sitting on her bed just as now when suddenly the telephone rang. She lifted the receiver and heard Farid's voice. He was speaking unusually fast.

'I'm speaking from home. Something urgent's come up. Can you get me some money?'

'I've got ten pounds,' she replied.

'I need a hundred,' he had said quickly.

'When?' she asked.

'Today or tomorrow at the latest.'

It was the first time Farid had asked her for anything, the first time anyone had asked her for anything. That day, she had been ill, with a splitting headache and couldn't move from bed, but suddenly her strength returned, she sat up and stared at the wall. It seemed to her that she was able to get up and search for that hundred pounds. Quickly she got up and dressed, not knowing from where she would get the money, only that she must go out and look for it. In a daze she wandered the streets, ideas rushed through her head – from relying on God to stealing and killing. Finally, she thought of her mother and hurried back home.

To get money from her mother was not easy, and only after inventing a big lie, which made her think her daughter's life

43

depended on those hundred pounds, did she succeed. Those were historic moments, the moments Fouada put the money into her bag and rushed over to Farid's house. When he opened the door, she was shaking and panting. She hurriedly opened her bag and put a hundred pounds on the desk without speaking, overflowing with happiness.

Yes, she was happy. Perhaps it was the happiest moment in her life, to be able to do something for Farid, to be able to do something for someone, something useful. Farid looked at her with brown, shining eyes in which she saw that strange thing she loved but did not understand.

'Thank you, Fouada,' he said and put his arms around her. Instead of kissing her on the mouth, as he did every time they met in the house, he kissed her gently on her forehead and turned away quickly, saying:

'I must go now.'

Fouada cried that night when she got home. Couldn't he have stayed with her five minutes longer? Was he too busy even to kiss her? What could be so important to him?

Part Two

She sat on an old chair in the living-room. The landlord sat opposite her. Between them stood the shabby table, on it a tray with two small coffee cups. His face was large and fleshy, a face one mistrusts the first time one sees it, something in the movement of the lips or eyes or something inexplicable giving it the appearance of lying or of deceit. Maybe it was that continuous, involuntary darting of his prominent eyes or the light tremor of his lips when he opened them to voice his rapid, mumbled words. She did not know exactly.

But should she judge people by their looks? Didn't she possess a scientific mind? Should she judge people according to her feelings and impressions of them? Why didn't she stop this foolish habit?

She saw his thin upper lip quiver as he spoke, revealing large yellow teeth.

'The rent of this apartment today is no less than thirty pounds a month,' he was saying.

She reached for a cup of coffee and said:

'I know, I know, but I only have two hundred. I'll pay it to you without taking the furniture. I don't need it.'

His bulging eyes flickered under his thick glasses, reminding her of a large fish under water. He glanced briefly at the caretaker standing by the door, then said:

'If you don't need the furniture, I'll reduce it to four hundred pounds.'

Swallowing a mouthful of bitter coffee, she said:

'I told you, I only have two hundred.'

Looking meekly at his master, the caretaker said:

'Please sir, she could pay two hundred now and the rest in instalments.'

The thin lips tightened into a smile and his fish-like eyes quivered as he said:

'All right, how much is each instalment?'

Fouada knew nothing about such dealings. She wanted the apartment; indeed, it had become the only hope in her life, almost the only salvation from that loss, that void; the only firm thread that might lead her to chemical research – perhaps to a great discovery. But this large fleshy face, those bulging eyes looking at her hungrily as if she were a piece of meat, would they be content with two hundred pounds in return for nothing? How would she pay off the rest? She would need to buy instruments and equipment in instalments. Where would she get it all? Then she had to pay the rent for the apartment every month and hire someone to receive clients and help clean the laboratory.

She hung her head, thinking in silence. Suddenly, she looked up at him. He was staring at her legs, greedily, and she automatically pulled her skirt down to cover her knees.

'I can't pay anything in instalments,' she said, picking up her bag and getting up to leave. He also got up and, as if embarrassed, looked down at the ground, mumbling in regret:

'I've never reduced the sum below five hundred for anyone and many people have come to me, but I refused to let the apartment for a long time. It's the best apartment in the building.'

'Yes, it is a nice apartment,' she said, making for the door, 'but I can't pay more than two hundred pounds.'

She walked towards the lift, feeling his glance burning her back. He opened the lift door for her and she went in, he behind her. He was large and broad-shouldered, with a prominent stomach and small feet. Before the lift descended, he said to the caretaker:

'Close up the apartment, Othman.'

The lift took them down. She saw his eyes examine her bust as though he were appraising it. She folded her arms over her chest and occupied herself by looking in the mirror. She was taken aback to see her own face. She hadn't seen it for a while, didn't recall having looked in the mirror for the past two days,

48

since Farid's disappearance. She had perhaps glanced at her hair when combing it, but hadn't noticed her face. Now it looked longer than ever, the eyes even wider, the whites shot with red. Her nose was still the same, her mouth too, with that ugly, involuntary gap. She closed her lips and swallowed hard. The lift came to a stop on the ground floor. She was conscious of the landlord still studying her from behind his thick glasses. She opened the lift door and was rushing out of the building when she heard his voice behind her saying:

'If you please, miss . . .'

When she turned to him, he continued:

'I don't know why you want the apartment . . . to live in?'

'No,' she said in annoyance, 'to turn into a chemical laboratory.'

His upper lip again uncovered his large, yellow teeth and he said:

'That's wonderful. Is it you who will work in it?'

'Yes,' she replied.

His eyes flickered briefly, then he said:

'I'd like to give you the apartment, but . . .'

'Thank you,' she interrupted him, 'but as I told you, I only have two hundred pounds.'

He gazed at her for a moment.

'I'll take two hundred. You can be sure I would never accept it from anyone else.'

She looked at him in surprise and said:

'Does that mean you agree?'

He gave her a weak smile, his protuberant eyes – like those of a frog – swimming behind his glasses, then said:

'Only to do you a favour.'

Hiding her joy, she said:

'Can I pay you now?'

'If you like,' he replied.

She opened her bag and handed him two hundred pounds.

'When shall I sign the lease?'

'Whenever you like,' he said.

49

'Now?'

'Now,' he answered.

*   *   *

Fouada left the building and walked down the street grave-faced. She was overcome by unreal, dreamlike feelings, a mixture of total disbelief at getting the apartment and extreme fear of losing it; the fear one experiences on acquiring something valuable, thinking that one might lose it at the very moment of possessing it.

It seemed that what had happened was only a dream. She opened her bag and saw the lease folded under her purse. She took it out and unfolded it, pausing to look at some of the words: the first party, Mohammed Saati; the second party, Fouada Khalil Salim. Reassured that it was indeed real, she folded the paper, put it back in her bag and continued walking.

Something heavy lay on her heart. What was it that weighed her down? Wasn't she supposed to be happy? Hadn't she got the apartment? Hadn't her hope been fulfilled? Wouldn't she now have her own chemical laboratory? Be able to do research? Try to make her discovery? Yes, she should be happy, but her heart was heavy as though weighed down by a stone.

She had no desire to go home, and let her feet take her where they would. Then she saw a telephone, behind a glass door; pushing it open, she went in and was about to lift the receiver when a gruff voice said: 'You can't use the phone.' She went out to look for another telephone. It was one o'clock, Friday. Maybe Farid had come back, but in her heart she knew she would not find him. That uninterrupted, loud ringing was all she would hear. It was better not to call, better to stop asking about him. He had left her, had vanished, so why burden her heart with cares?

She saw a telephone in a cigarette kiosk and, pretending not to notice it, walked by, but then turned back and lifted the receiver with cold, trembling fingers.

The ringing tone pierced her head like a sharp instrument. It hurt her ear but she pressed the receiver closer, as if enjoying

50

the pain, as if it was curing another greater and heavier pain, like someone who cauterizes their flesh with hot irons to rid themselves of a pain in the liver or spleen. The receiver remained pressed against her ear, seemingly stuck to it, until she heard the vendor say:

'Other people want to use the telephone too . . .'

She put down the receiver and continued on her way, head bowed. Where had he vanished? Why hadn't he told her the truth? Had it all been a deception? Had all her feelings been a lie? Why couldn't she stop thinking about him? How long would she roam the streets? What was the point of this futile, circling around like the hands of a clock? Should she not start buying instruments and equipment for the laboratory?

Raising her head, she saw a back that looked like Farid's. She stood rooted to the spot as though paralysed by an electrical current. But when she saw the man's face, in profile, she relaxed: it was not Farid. Her muscles seemed flaccid as they do after an electric shock; she felt unable to walk, that her legs were powerless to support her. Nearby was a small café with tables on the pavement, so she sat down on one of the chairs and glanced around her, half conscious. Everything seemed familiar. Hadn't she seen it all before? The lame old man distributing lottery tickets? The dark-skinned waiter with the deep scar on his chin? The oblong marble table on which she laid her hand? The little, fat man at the next table drinking coffee, the thin brown lines on the cup? Even the tremor of the man's hand as he raised the cup to his mouth? All this had happened before. But she had never sat in this café, had never even been in this street . . . but sitting there . . . the lame old man, the waiter, the table, everything . . . had surely happened once before, she didn't know where or when . . .

She recalled having once read something about reincarnation and sceptically told herself that perhaps she had lived before in another body.

At that moment, a strange thought strayed into her mind: she would see Farid pass by in the street in front of her. It was more than a thought, an idea, it was a conviction. It even seemed that some hidden force had brought her to this particular café, in this particular street, at this particular moment, precisely in order to see Farid.

She did not believe in hidden spirits. Her mind was scientific and believed only in what could be put to analysis and into a test tube. But this unbidden conviction so dominated her that she trembled with fear, imagining that the moment she saw Farid she would fall to the ground struck by belief, like a blow from an invisible hand.

She tensed the muscles of her face and body, ready for the blow that would fall the moment she saw Farid walking amongst the people. Unblinking, her eyes scoured the faces of passers-by, her breath bated, her heart pounding violently as if to empty out its last drop.

The moment passed; she did not see Farid. She gulped, some calm restored, thanking God that he had not appeared, that she had not been struck down. Then she began to feel anxious that the prediction had not been fulfilled, that she would again fall into the abyss of waiting, of searching. She still hoped she would see him and went on staring into men's faces, scrutinizing each one. Some shared a feature or movement with Farid, and her eyes would settle momentarily on some similarity as though seeing a real part of Farid.

It was some time before Fouada became certain that her strange conviction was false. Her head and neck muscles slackened in disappointment, but also a faint relief crept upon her, the kind of relief that follows a release from responsibilities and belief.

*   *   *

Five days later, the laboratory was ready. It was Tuesday afternoon and Fouada was walking down Qasr al-Nil Street towards the laboratory carrying a package of test tubes and thin rubber tubing. She paused on the pavement waiting with others for the signal to cross the road.

Waiting for the green light, she looked up at the façade of the building opposite. Windows, balconies, doorways and spaces

52

on the walls were covered with hoardings – bearing the names of doctors, lawyers, accountants, tailors, masseuses and other private professionals. The names, in large black letters on a white background, looked, she thought, like the obituary page in a newspaper. She saw her name – Fouada Khalil Salim – in black letters at the top of one page . . . and her heart shuddered, as though what she read was the notice of her own death. But she knew she hadn't died; she was standing at the traffic lights, waiting for them to turn green, she could move her arms. As she swung her arms, one of them struck a man standing beside her with three other men. They were all looking at the front of the building, reading the hoardings. She imagined they were looking at her name in particular and shrank into her coat in embarrassment. It seemed to her that her name was no longer spelt out in letters of black paint but something intimate – like limbs – like the limbs of her body. With the eyes of the men examining her exposed name, she felt, in a confused way, that they were examining her naked body displayed in a window. When the lights changed, she slipped in amongst the other pedestrians to hide, remembering an incident from her first year in primary school. The teacher of religion, his nose thick and curved like the beak of a bird, stood before the class of young girls aged between six and eight expounding the religious teaching which stipulated feminine modesty. That day he said that a female must cover her body because it was private and she must not speak in the presence of strange men because even her voice was private. He also said that her name was private and should not be spoken out loud in front of strange men. He gave an example, saying: 'When, and only in extreme necessity, I have to mention my wife in the presence of men, I never utter her real name.'

Fouada, the young child, listened without understanding a word of what he said but instead read the teacher's features as he spoke. When he said the word 'private', she didn't understand what it meant, but she felt from his expression that it meant something ugly and obscene, and she shrank into her chair, grieving for her female self. The day might have passed peacefully, like any other day, but the teacher of religion decided to ask her the meaning of what he had said . . . She got to her feet trembling with fear and, as she stood, she did not know how, urine involuntarily ran down between her legs. The eyes of all the girls turned to her wet legs, she wanted to cry but was too ashamed.

*   *   *

Fouada was in her chemical laboratory. Everything around her was new, washed and waiting: the pipes, the test tubes, the equipment, the basins, everything. She went over to the microscope placed on its own table with its own light, and turned the knob, looking down the lens. She saw a clean and empty circle of light and said to herself:

'Maybe one day, in this circle, I will find the object of my long search.'

She felt a desire to work, so she put on a white overall, fixed the pipes and lit the gas burner. The softly hissing light of the flame was brilliant and she picked up a test tube with metal pincers, washed it carefully so that no speck of dust should remain and put it to the tongue of the flame to dry, then braced herself for the research.

But she remained motionless, holding the empty test tube, staring into it as if she had forgotten the object of the research, feeling cold sweat creep across her forehead. A fundamental question suddenly hit her, a question to which she had always known the answer; but when she actually faced it and began to think, the answer escaped her. The more she thought, the further it escaped. She recalled the day a colleague had read her coffee cup to predict future events. The friend reading the cup suddenly asked her:

'What's your mother's name?'

Startled by the unexpected question Fouada was taken aback. She couldn't remember her mother's name. Her friend insisted, and the more she pressed, the further away the name escaped Fouada's memory till, in the end, the reading had to continue without it. But Fouada remembered the name at the very moment the friend stopped asking.

54

She continued to stare into the empty test tube. Then she put it back on the rack and began to pace the room, her head bowed. Everything could disappear except that! Everything could escape her except that! For that to vanish was intolerable, unbearable! It was all she had left, the only reason for her to continue living.

She went over to the window and opened it. Cold air struck her face and she felt somewhat refreshed. 'It's depression,' she thought. 'I shouldn't think about research when I'm depressed.' She looked out of the window. The large sign hung from the railing of the balcony. The street was far below and people were going on their way without looking up, paying no attention to her chemical laboratory. It seemed that nobody would be interested in her laboratory, that nobody would knock at her door. She chewed her lips in anxiety and was about to close the window when she noticed a woman standing below and looking up at her window. All at once, she became excited. No doubt the woman was suffering from gout and had come for a urine analysis. She rushed to the outer room, on the door of which was written 'Waiting Room', and straightened the chairs. She looked at herself in the long mirror near the door and saw the white overall reaching to above her knees like a hairdressers, glanced over her gaping mouth and looked into her eyes, smiling as she whispered to herself:

'Fouada Khalil Salim, owner of a chemical analysis laboratory. Yes, it's me.'

She heard the drone of the lift come to a stop, heard its door open and close, heard the clacking of heavy high heels on the tiled floor of the corridor. Fouada waited behind the door for the sound of the bell, but heard nothing. Very quietly, she slid back the peep-hole and saw a woman's back disappearing through the door of the neighbouring apartment. She read the small copper plaque on the door: 'Shalabi's Sport Institute for Slimming and Massage'.

She closed the peep-hole and went back into the inner room on the door of which was written: 'Research and Analysis Room'. She avoided looking at the empty test tubes and began pacing up and down the room, then looked at the time. It was eight. Remembering that today was Tuesday, she threw off the overall, flung it on to a chair, then rushed out.

Last Tuesday he had not come – perhaps for an unavoidable reason? And here was another Tuesday. Would he come today? Would she go to the restaurant and find him sitting at the table? His back towards her, his face towards the Nile? Her heart pounded but inside it was that weight that hardened and contracted like a ball of lead. She would not find him, so why go to the restaurant? She tried to turn and head for home but couldn't. Involuntarily, her feet made for the restaurant like a wild horse that has thrown its rider and is galloping unrestrained.

She saw the naked table-top, the air whipping it from all sides like a rock in a violent and tempestuous sea. She stood for a moment grave-faced, then left the restaurant with head bowed and made her way home with slow and heavy steps.

* * *

Her mother was in the corner of the living-room praying, back to the door and face to the wall. Fouada stood looking at her. Her bowed back was bent forward, the raised hem of her robe exposed the back of her legs. She knelt on the ground for a few moments, then got to her feet and bent forward again, lifting her robe and uncovering her legs. Fouada saw large, blue veins protruding from the back of her legs like long winding worms and said to herself: 'A serious heart or artery condition.' Her mother knelt on the ground, turned her head to the right and whispered something, then looked to the left muttering the same words. Finally, she stood up supporting herself on the sofa, put her feet into her slippers and turned to Fouada standing behind her.

'In the Name of Allah, the Compassionate, the Merciful!' she intoned. 'When did you come in?'

'Just now,' Fouada replied, sitting on the sofa and sighing with fatigue. The mother sat down beside her and looking at her said:

'You seem tired.'

She was just about to say very tired, but glancing at her

56

mother's face and seeing the whites of her large eyes, clearly tinged with a yellowness she had never seen before, said:

'I've been working hard. Are you tired, mama?'

'Me, tired?' said her mother in surprise.

'Your heart, for example,' Fouada replied.

'Why?' her mother said.

'I noticed varicose veins in your legs when you were praying,' she said.

'What's the heart got to do with legs?'

'The blood goes to the legs from the heart,' she replied.

Her mother waved her hand dismissively.

'It can go where it likes,' she said, 'I don't feel tired.'

'Sometimes we don't feel tired,' Fouada said, 'but the illness is hidden in our bodies. It might be as well to do an examination.'

Crossing her legs her mother said:

'I detest doctors.'

'You don't have to go to a doctor,' Fouada said. 'I'll carry out an examination . . .'

'What examination?' her mother said in alarm.

'I'll take a urine sample and analyse it in my laboratory,' she replied.

Her mother gave a wry smile and exclaimed:

'Ah, I understand! You want to carry out an experiment on me!'

Fouada stared at her for a moment, then said:

'What experiment? I'm offering you a free service.'

'Thank you very much,' her mother said, 'I'm in the best of health and I don't want to delude myself that I'm ill.'

'It's neither a matter of delusion, mama,' Fouada said in annoyance, 'nor of illness.'

'So what's the point of analysis then?'

'Confirming the absence of illness is one thing, analysis is something else,' she replied.

She fell silent for a moment, then more quietly said:

'Analysis in itself is an art which I take pleasure in performing.'

Her mother's upper lip curled in derision:

'What's the art or pleasure in analysing urine?'

As if talking to herself, Fouada replied:

'It's work that relies on the senses, just like art.'

'What senses?' asked her mother.

'Smell, touch, sight, taste . . .' Fouada said.

'Taste?' her mother exclaimed, staring at her daughter for a moment.

'It seems to me you know nothing about these analyses!' she said.

Fouada looked at her mother and saw a strange look in her eyes, like that in her wedding photograph, a hard, suspicious look, bitterly mistrustful of whoever was before her. She felt the blood rush to her head and found herself saying:

'I know why you refuse. You refuse because you don't believe in analysis.'

Without meaning to, she raised her voice and shouted:

'You don't believe that I can do anything. That was always your opinion of me, that was always your opinion of father . . .'

Her mother's mouth fell open in surprise.

'What are you saying?'

Raising her voice even louder, she replied:

'No, you don't believe in me. That's a fact which you've always tried to hide from me.'

Her mother gazed at her in utter astonishment and in a feeble voice said:

'And why shouldn't I believe in you . . . ?'

'Because I'm your daughter,' Fouada shouted. 'People never appreciate the things that they have simply because they have them.'

Fouada lowered her head, holding it in her hands as if she had a bad headache. The mother kept staring at her, silent and apprehensive.

'Who told you that I don't believe in you, daughter?' she said sadly. 'If only you knew how I felt when I saw you for the first time after you were born. You lay beside me like a little angel, breathing quietly and looking around in wonder with your small shining eyes. I picked you up, lifted you to show you to your father and said to him: "Just look at her, Khalil." Your father glanced at you briefly, then said angrily: "It's a girl." Raising you up to his face, I said to him: "She'll be a great woman, Khalil. Look at her eyes! Kiss her, Khalil! Kiss her!" I held you so that your face almost touched his, but he didn't kiss you, just turned away and left us . . .'

The mother wiped away a tear from her eye on her sleeve, and continued:

'That night I hated him more than ever. I stayed awake the whole night looking at your tiny face as you slept. Whenever I put my finger in your hand, you wrapped your little fingers around it and held on tightly. I cried till daybreak. I don't know, daughter, what illness I had but my temperature suddenly rose and I fainted . . . when I came round, I found I'd been taken to hospital where they removed my womb and I became sterile.'

She took a handkerchief from the pocket of her *galabiyya* to wipe away the tears which ran down her face, and said:

'You were the only thing I had in my life. I used to go into your room when you were up at night studying and say to you . . .'

She was weeping and put the handkerchief to her eyes for a moment, then lifted it and said:

'Have you forgotten, Fouada?'

Fouada was fighting off a sharp pain in the side of her head and was silent and distracted, as if half asleep.

'I haven't forgotten, mama,' she said faintly.

Gently, her mother asked:

'What did I used to say to you, Fouada?'

'You used to tell me that you believed that I would succeed and do better than all my friends . . .'

Her mother's dry lips parted in a weak smile and she said:

'You see? I always believed in you.'

'You only imagined I was better than all the other girls.'

'I didn't only imagine it,' said her mother with conviction. 'I was sure of it.'

Fouada looked into her mother's eyes and said:

'Why were you so sure?'

'Just like that, for no reason . . .' she responded quickly.

Fouada tried to read the expression in her mother's eyes so as to understand, to discover the secret of that conviction which lay in them, but she saw nothing. In a flash, she felt her irritation grow into anger and snapped at her mother:

'That conviction ruined my life . . . !'

'What . . . !' her mother exclaimed in astonishment.

Without thinking and as if her words were dictated by someone from the distant past, she said:

'That conviction of yours haunted me like a ghost. It weighed me down. I only passed my exams . . .'

She paused for a moment, looking around distractedly, then gulped, then went on, speaking quickly:

'Yes, only passed my exams for your sake. It used to torture me, yes, torture me because I loved science and I could have passed by myself . . .' She put her head in her hands and pressed it hard.

Her mother was silent for a moment, then said sadly:

'You're depressed tonight, Fouada. What's been happening these past few days? You're not your usual self.'

Fouada remained silent, clutching her head in both hands as if fearing it would snap. A sharp pain split her head in two, while somewhere at the back something pointed made itself felt. She didn't know what it was exactly, but it seemed to begin to disclose the true reason for the mysterious sadness which sometimes came over her just when she'd had a happy moment.

And that reason was none other than her mother. She loved her mother more than anything else, more than Farid, more than chemistry, more than discovery, more than her very self. She was incapable of freeing herself from this love even though she wanted to, as though she had fallen into an eternal trap whose chains and ropes bound her legs and hands – from which she would never in all her life be able to release herself.

Unconsciously, she moved her little finger, ran it over her upper lip, then put it in her mouth. She began to chew it like a child whose teeth have emerged but who is still sucking its mother's breast. A long time elapsed as she sat on the sofa in the living-room, her head between her hands, the tip of her little finger between her teeth. Her mother seemed to have left the room and she didn't know where she'd gone, but after a while she returned holding a small glass of yellow liquid. She extended the slender, veined hand that held the glass to her daughter. Fouada raised her eyes to her and the pent-up tears fell from them into her lap.

*   *   *

Fouada took great delight in washing the tubes, preparing flasks of alkalis and acids, checking the chemical analysis equipment and the spectrometer. She lit the burner, poured a sample of her mother's urine into the test tube and held it in a metal clamp over the flame. Standing like this, she realized why she had suggested that her mother give her a sample: she had wanted to use the new laboratory equipment.

The sample was free of sediment and since the heat solidified nothing, she turned off the burner, poured a drop of cold urine on to a slide which she placed under the microscope, and looked down the lens. She saw a large circle inside within which moved small discs of different shapes and sizes. She moved the mirror to adjust the light and turned the knob of the magnifying lens. The large circle widened, increasing her field of vision, and the small quivering discs became bigger and looked like grapes floating on water.

She focused on one of the discs. It had, she thought, the form of an ovule. It was shaking like a living creature and inside it quivered two small dark discs, like a pair of eyes. As she stared at them her conscious, scientific mind was suspended and it seemed to her that they stared back at her with her mother's familiar look. Like an ovule – it was her mother's . . . perhaps she herself was this ovule thirty years previously . . . only her mother had not put it into a test tube and closed it with a stopper. It had attached itself to her flesh like a louse to the scalp and had eaten her cells and sucked her blood.

She remained, unmoving, like a dreamer, staring into the lens, time and thought lost as her imagination ran riot. She

61

pictured, with shock and disbelief, her mother lying on a bed with her father beside her. She had never before imagined that her mother performed those acts that women did before having children, although certainly her mother had performed them, the proof being her own existence. She imagined her mother's form in such a position and pictured her the way she knew her, with a white scarf wrapped around her head, a long *galabiyya* over her body, long black socks on her feet and woollen slippers too. Yes, she saw her in all these things lying on the bed in her father's arms, her lips sternly closed, a grave frown on her wide forehead, performing her marital duty – slowly and with the same dignified movements with which she performed her prayers.

The door bell was ringing. It had been ringing ever since she saw the 'ovule'. Dazed, she thought at first it was the bell of the next door apartment or of a bicycle in the street. But it went on ringing. She left the microscope and went to open the door.

The dark discs were still quivering before her eyes when she saw a pair of bulging eyes inside which darted two prominent black pupils. It seemed to her she was still looking down the microscope and she passed her hand over her eyes saying:

'Come in, Mr Saati.'

His massive bulk followed her into the waiting-room with hesitant steps as if he didn't know why he had come. Looking around at the new metal chairs, he said:

'Congratulations! Congratulations! What a very nice laboratory.'

He sat down on one of the chairs, saying:

'I thought about calling in on you several times before today to congratulate you on the new laboratory, but I was afraid . . .'

He fell silent for a moment, his eyes uncertain behind his thick glasses, then he went on:

'. . . I was afraid of disturbing you.'

'Thank you,' she said quietly.

Looking up, he saw the copper plaque and exclaimed:

'Research Room!' He got up, put his head round the door of the room and saw the new materials, test tubes and bowls and said admiringly:

'It's wonderful, wonderful! It really is a chemical laboratory!'

She looked around somewhat surprised. She hadn't yet felt that she really possessed a laboratory or that it was a real chemistry laboratory. It seemed incomplete to her, many things were lacking. In genuine surprise she exclaimed:

'Honestly? Does it really look like a chemical laboratory to you?'

He looked at her in surprise.

'And you? Doesn't it look that way to you?'

Regarding her laboratory with new eyes, she said absently:

'We don't always see the things we have.'

He smiled, drawing back his upper lip and again revealing large, yellow teeth, and said:

'That's true, especially in the case of husbands and wives.'

He gave a short laugh, then sat down again on his chair while she remained standing.

'You seem to be busy. Am I holding you back?' he asked her.

She sat down on a chair near the door.

'I was doing some research,' she said.

She smiled for no reason, perhaps remembering the shape of her mother's ovule. His intimate glances devoured her face and he said:

'I'll tell you something. Do you know you look like my daughter? The same smile, eyes, figure, everything . . .'

Fouada felt his gaze on her body and looked down in silence. To herself she whispered:

'He only wants to chat.'

'When I saw you for the first time,' he said, 'I felt that curious resemblance, felt I knew you . . . maybe that's why I decided to give you the apartment.'

Yes, he just wanted to chat. Now he was talking about the apartment. What had brought him here? He had ruined her pleasure in analysing her mother's urine.

'In the past few days,' he continued, 'I thought about coming to help you prepare the laboratory, but I was worried that you

63

might think badly of me. Women here think badly of a man who shows a desire to help, don't they?'

She was silent, suddenly preoccupied with something else, recalling an incident from her childhood when she played in the street with other children. There was a foolish old man who used to wander the streets and the children ran after him chanting: 'The idiot's here!' She would run with the other children and chant with them. One day, she ran faster than the others, leaving them behind and catching up with him. The old man spun round and gave her such a fearsome look that she turned on her heels and, imagining that he would chase and catch her, ran like the wind. From that day, she stopped chasing him with the other children and hid when she saw him, for it seemed to her that his fearsome, terrifying glance was for her alone.

Fouada couldn't think why she now remembered that distant incident, except that the eyes of the foolish old man had bulged like these in front of her. She looked around the laboratory as if suddenly discovering that she was alone with Saati in the apartment. Feeling frightened, she got up and said:

'I must leave now. I've just remembered something important.'

He got up saying:

'Sorry for interrupting you. Would you like a lift somewhere in my car?'

She rushed over to the door and opened it.

'No, thank you, it's not far.'

He went out and she locked the apartment and went ahead of him to go down by the stairs. In surprise, he said to her:

'Aren't you waiting for the lift?'

'I prefer to walk,' she replied, rushing down the stairs.

*　　*　　*

She walked along the street looking in the shop windows. Darkness was falling fast, the street and shop lights were already lit and she had no wish to go home. Walking alone, she peered searchingly into the faces of those who passed by, already addicted to this strange habit, the habit of comparing men, their features, their movements, their size, to Farid. She was also addicted to something even more bizarre: making predictions and then being convinced of the possibility of them coming true. As she walked along the street, she might tell herself: 'Three private cars will pass followed by a taxi. I shall look into the taxi and see Farid sitting there.' Then she'd start counting the passing cars and when the prediction was not borne out she'd bite her upper lip and say: 'Who said it would come true anyway? It's nothing but an illusion.' She'd go on her way and in a while, another, different prediction would occur to her.

At the end of Qasr al-Nil Street, a crowd had gathered around a car. She heard a voice say: 'A man's dead.' She found herself pushing through, panting and trembling, until she reached the man lying on the ground. She looked at his face. It was not Farid. Slowly, heavily she made her way out of the crowd.

She left Qasr al-Nil Street and headed for Suleiman Street. It was bustling with people, but she saw no one. Her thoughts were far away, perceiving the bodies around her only as part of the exterior boundaries that separated her from the vast, pulsating mass of the world, and knowing instinctively that such a body occupied such a sector of the street and that she must avoid colliding with it.

Then it seemed that some obstruction stood in her way. She raised her head to find a long queue of people across the street; and so she stopped too.

The queue gradually moved forward until she found herself in front of a ticket office. She bought a ticket and with the others went towards a large door in a dark hall. Torchlight was shone on to her ticket and she followed its circle of light until she reached a seat.

A film had just begun. On the screen, a man and a woman were embracing on a bed. The camera drew away from them to a man's foot showing from beneath the bed, then returned to the man and the woman who were still joined in a long kiss. Something crawled up Fouada's leg and, without taking her eyes off the screen, she brushed it away.

65

On screen the kiss ended and the man dressed and left. The woman said something, the other man came out from under the bed and the embracing began anew.

She sensed the crawling again. It didn't feel like a fly, more like a cockroach, for it did not flit around but crept slowly up her leg. Eager not to miss any of the film, she kept her eyes on the screen, reaching out in the dark to catch the insect before it climbed above her knee. But her fingers closed around something solid and in terror she looked at her hand to find that she had grabbed the finger of the man sitting next to her. She held on to his finger, glowering at him angrily. But he didn't turn to her, just kept looking at the screen in total absorption as if he did not see her, and as if his finger were nothing to do with him. She threw his finger into his face so that it almost jabbed him in the eye, but he continued to stare at the screen as though sleeping. She stumbled quickly to her feet and left the cinema.

*   *   *

Stretched out on her bed she stared at the ceiling, at that familiar, small, jagged circle where the layer of white paint had fallen. Feeling cold, she pulled up the covers and closed her eyes to sleep, but did not sleep. She considered reaching for the telephone . . . to dial those five numbers as she did every night before going to sleep, but she kept her hand still and pressed her head into the pillow, saying: 'I must stop this habit.' But she didn't stop. She knew there would be only that cold, shrilling bell, which had ceased to be a sound or air waves and become barbed fragments of metal that penetrated her ear, that seared like fire.

And yet she had grown used to it. At the same time every night she dialled the same five numbers, pressed her ear to the receiver and invited that searing pain as if it comforted her, like a sick person cauterizing their body with fire to stifle another, more intense fire, or like an addict grown dependent on the taste of a poison who demands it every day.

The sound of the bell, the sound of her sobs, her sighs and heartbeats intermingled, indistinguishably. A conglomerate that

66

manifested itself as one continuous, penetrating whistle like that which rings in the ears when there is total silence.

Very well! She waited for the bell every night as if it had become a new lover. She knew it was only a bell, but it came from Farid's telephone, rang in Farid's house, vibrated on Farid's desk at which they had often sat beside each other, reverberated against the divan on which they had often lain together, and moved the air which they had breathed in together and exhaled together.

The bell stopped. Farid's voice whispered in her ear. She felt his arm around her waist, his warm breath on her neck. She had not forgotten that he had been away from her so long, and yet she seemed unaware of everything, could remember nothing, not even that she had a head or arms or legs. All her senses had flowed away and all that was left of her were two swollen, inflamed lips.

She opened her eyes to look into his. But it was not Farid. It was another man with small blue eyes and thick eyebrows. The first man she had ever loved. She was a young child, she didn't recall how old she was at the time, but she did remember that as she grew older, she would open her eyes every morning to find her bed dry. She had hated being wet and thanked God that it was over. But God was not deceived by her thanks and soon afflicted her with another type of wetness, even more serious, for it was not colourless like before and had no sooner dried than it soaked the white bed sheet again. No, it was deep red and could be removed only by scrubbing so hard that her small fingers burned and then, even after washing, it did not disappear completely but left a pale yellow stain.

She didn't know the real reason for it, for it was a haphazard wetness that appeared and disappeared as it pleased. She believed that somebody attacked her small body while she slept or that on her alone had fallen some malignant disease. She hid the catastrophe of her body from her mother and thought of going to the doctor on her own to reveal her secret. But once, her mother caught her washing the bedsheet at the sink. She was so ashamed that the earth spun and she tried to roll the sheet up.

She saw her mother's eyes looking at her from under a shadow she had never seen before. She reached out for the sheet and took it from her and saw the red patch on the white fabric, lying there like a dead cockroach. She tried to deny her disgraceful crime but her mother seemed to collude in it with her and was neither shocked nor angry, nor even surprised. It was as if she expected this misfortune to befall her and accepted it calmly and completely.

Fouada mistrusted this calm. It even terrified her, so much that her body trembled. So it was not a catastrophe. So it was not a unique, temporary sickness. It was something ordinary, quite ordinary. Her terror increased as her sense of its ordinariness grew. She had hoped it was something unique since unique things are bearable precisely because they are unique and not permanent.

Her small body began to change. She felt the change flow through her like a soft snake with a long, thin tail that flicked and flickered in her chest and stomach, stinging different parts of her body. The stings were both painful and pleasurable. How, she wondered, could these physical sensations be painful and pleasurable at one and the same time? But her body seemed to be wiser than she and was content with the pain and with the pleasure, happy with both side by side, embracing both with neither wonder nor surprise.

Her body changed suddenly and yet gradually. She felt and did not feel the change, like warm air entering her nose, or tepid water quietly pouring over her, which she bore without feeling its warmth since it was the same temperature as her blood.

She was surprised one day when she saw her naked breasts in the mirror. There was no longer the smooth chest she was used to seeing but instead two peaks, tipped by two dark raisins, that rose and fell with every breath, that jumped when she jumped as though, were it not for that thin layer of skin, they would fall off like oranges fall from a tree.

When she jumped, she felt something else jump behind her. She turned before the mirror to discover two other rounded humps held taut by fleshy skin at the lower part of her back. She remained studying her body for a while. It seemed to her to be that of some other girl, not Fouada, or that of an adult woman. She felt ashamed to look at those curves and protrusions that flaunted themselves disgracefully with every breath. But there was something besides shame, something deep and buried, something that wrapped itself in a thick mist, something like hidden pleasure or wicked pride.

Why did these old images stay in her mind alongside the image of the first man? Why did they persist when other more significant and more recent images had gone? But she believed that a chemical reaction happened in the memory cells, dissolving some images and highlighting or distorting others so that some parts remained whilst others were effaced. Yes, parts were eliminated. The lower half of the body of the first man in her life was effaced. Why? She didn't remember him having a lower half. He had a large head, small blue eyes, shoulders and long arms. How did he walk without legs? She didn't remember ever seeing him walk, for he was always at the window of his room. Taller people might have been able to see inside the room as they passed by in the street but she was small and could see only if she jumped up.

She deliberately played with her skipping rope under his window and every time she skipped, she would peek into the room. She could not see everything clearly because her head went down too quickly but she did manage to glimpse a painting hanging on the wall, a large suitcase on top of the wardrobe, a desk with books on it. She loved the coloured painting more than anything else and jumping under the window one day, said to him:

'I want a coloured painting.'

'Come in and I'll give you a painting,' he said to her.

She could not go without her mother's permission, and her mother refused, saying firmly:

'You're too old to skip in the street.'

She threw herself on to her bed, shaking with rage. She hated her mother at that moment and envied her friend Saadia whose mother had died in childbirth. But she soon got up and tiptoed out, shoes in hand, and ran into the street.

Her heart was racing as she knocked at his door. She was happy because she would get a coloured painting, but she knew that the picture was not the sole reason for her happiness. She wanted to see his room from inside, wanted to see the shape of his wardrobe, his bed, his slippers. She wanted to touch his books and papers and pictures, wanted to touch everything.

He opened the door and she entered, out of breath. She stood by the wall shivering like a plucked chicken. He spoke to her but her voice was stifled and she could not answer. He came over to her and she saw his blue eyes close to her. She felt afraid. Close up, the shape of his face was strange, a sharp look in his eyes like that of a wild cat. He pulled her towards him with his long arms and she screamed, fearing that he would slaughter or stifle her. He slapped her face saying: 'Don't scream!' but she only grew more scared and screamed all the more. While trying to escape from his arms, she heard a rap on the door. He let go of her to open it and she nearly fell to the ground. There stood her mother, flesh and blood, in the middle of the room.

She opened her eyes to find herself lying on the bed shivering with cold. It was dark and the window was open. She imagined a ghost moving behind the window and trembled, even though she knew it was only the eucalyptus tree shaken by gusts of wind. She got up to close the window, then went back to bed and got in under the blankets.

Thinking that she heard breathing other than her own in the room, she peered out from under the covers and looked fearfully around. Her eye fell on a long shadow standing beside her wardrobe and she was about to scream when she realized it was only the clothes-stand with her coat on it. She closed her eyes to sleep but then felt the movement of something that seemed to come from under the bed. She wanted to reach out and turn on the light but she was afraid to put her hand out in case the ghost crouching under the bed grabbed it and so she stayed curled up under the covers, wide-eyed, until sleep coursed through her body as warm as blood.

*   *   *

The rays of the sun were filtering through the slats of the shutter when Fouada awoke. She remained curled up under the covers, wanting to stay there for ever. But she got up and dragged her body over to the mirror. Her face was sallow and seemed even longer than usual, her eyes larger, her lips paler, between them that ever-widening gap that made her teeth appear even more prominent. She gazed into her eyes for a moment, as if searching for something, then pursed her lips in displeasure and went to the bathroom. She took a hot shower and, feeling refreshed, smiled as she looked at her body in the mirror. She was tall and slender, with long arms and legs, and felt a hidden power in her muscles, an unspent power, an imprisoned power, which she did not know how to release. She dressed and went out into the street. The air was fresh, the sun bright and warm, and every-thing sparkled and quivered with animation. She strode along swinging her arms briskly in the air, feeling strong and energetic and greeting the new day eagerly. But where was she going? To that putrid tomb which smelled of urine? To that shabby desk at which she sat for six hours a day doing nothing? Would that strength and that eagerness dissipate into nothing?

She saw a horse pulling a cart, its hooves striking the ground with strength and vigour. She stared at the horse in envy. It spent its power pulling the cart, it released its energy, moved its feet happily. If she were a horse, she would be the same, pulling her cart, clattering on the ground with her hooves, perfectly happy.

When bus 613 came, she stood still and looked at it, motionless like a stubborn horse. No, she would not go to the Ministry, would not waste the day on nothing, would not waste her life signing the attendance register. For what? For those few pounds she took home every month? Sell her life for a few pounds? Bury her intelligence in that closed room with its stagnant air? Yes, it was that stagnant air that dissipated her vigour, the stagnant air that shut off her thoughts, killed them before they were born. She often had thoughts, research ideas often occurred to her, she often came close to making a discovery, but everything withered away in that room with closed doors

71

and windows and sombre, dreary desks and those three mummified heads.

Another bus came. She almost got on but stood her ground and looked at it steadily. This moment came every day without her triumphing over it. If only she could manage today, she could manage every day. If only she could triumph once, that once would break the awful habit.

The bus was still there, but she stayed where she was and raised her head to the sky. Another moment and the bus would be gone without her and it would all be over. The sky would remain just as high and blue and silent. Nothing would happen. No, nothing would happen.

She took a deep breath and said aloud: 'Nothing will happen.' She put her hands into the pockets of her coat and walked off humming to herself. She looked about her in surprise and joy, like a prisoner emerging into the street for the first time after long years in prison. She saw a newspaper vendor, bought a paper and glanced at the headlines on the front page, then bit her lips. They were the same headlines she saw every day, the same faces, the same names. She looked at the date on the top of the page, thinking she was holding yesterday's paper or that of the previous week or year. She turned the pages, scanning them for a new subject or a new face but reached the last page without finding anything. She folded the newspaper and tucked it under her arm but then remembered having seen a familiar pair of bulging eyes in one of the pictures, eyes that looked like Saati's. She opened the paper again and, to her astonishment, her eye fell on the photograph of Saati himself. She read his name under the picture: Mohammed Saati, head of the Supreme Board for Building and Construction. Unconsciously, she ran her fingers over the eyes as if they protruded from the paper, even though the page was soft, smooth and flat.

She read the text under the photograph. It described in detail a meeting that Saati had held with the board workers, in words she seemed to have read so many times before. She had often read the name Saati and seen his picture. Fouada was amazed that she hadn't made the connection between all this and Saati the landlord whom she knew, but she never imagined that this same Saati could be the subject of an article in a newspaper. She looked again at the picture and the name, then folded the paper and put it under her arm.

The caretaker was sitting on his bench in the sun when she reached the building. He jumped to his feet when he saw her and ran towards her, holding out a small piece of white paper. She unfolded the paper to read: 'I will come by at six p.m. today. It's important. Saati.' As she entered the lift, her fingers toyed with the paper and unconsciously tore it to shreds which she then tossed through the iron grille of the lift.

He would come by at six in the evening. Something important. What could be so important? What could be important from her point of view? The matter of research? Where Farid was? The collapse of the Ministry building? That was her life. Nothing outside that was important. But Saati knew nothing about research or Farid or the Ministry, so what could be so important in his visit?

She entered the laboratory, put on the white overall, arranged the gleaming glasses and bowls on the table, lit the burner and grasped the metal clamp in order to pick up the test tube. But instead she left it in the wooden rack, upright, its empty mouth open to the air.

For some minutes, she gazed at the empty test tube, then sat down, head in her hands. Where to start? She didn't know, didn't know at all! Chemistry had evaporated from her head. Ideas crowded her mind when she read or carried out experiments in the college laboratory or whilst she walked in the street or slept. Where had all these ideas gone? They were in her head. Yes, they were there. she felt them move, heard their voices. A long conversation took place between them which culminated in results that surprised her.

She often arrived at a new idea that made her almost mad with joy. Yes, almost mad. She looked around in surprise and saw people walking as if they were beings of a species alien to her. And she? She was something else! In her head was something not in the head of anyone else, something that would dazzle the scientists, something that might change the world. A car or bus might almost hit her and she'd jump on to the pavement in fear and cautiously walk alongside a wall. Her life might be lost under some wheels and with it the new idea for ever. She walked faster, wanting to communicate the idea to the world before something happened to her, almost running, then really running and panting, then stopping and looking around her. Where, where was she running? She suddenly found that she didn't know, didn't know!

She turned off the burner, removed the white overall and went out into the street. The movement of her arms and legs relaxed her, relieved the pressure in her head, released that pent-up energy inside her. She noticed a telephone in a shop and stopped suddenly. Why didn't they put telephones in less obvious places? Why did they have to display them like this? If she hadn't seen the telephone, she wouldn't have remembered. She reached out and lifted the receiver, put her finger in a hole and began to dial. The bell echoed in her ear, sharp, loud and uninterrupted. Quietly, she replaced the receiver and took some steps, then stopped abruptly, saying to herself: 'Is it Farid? Is Farid's absence the reason? Why has everything changed? Why has everything become unbearable?' When Farid was present, her life was the same, only Farid made everything bearable. She would look into his shining, brown eyes and feel that worldly things were without value. The Ministry was transformed into a small antiquated building, research became just another empty illusion and discovery, yes, even discovery became another wan, childish dream.

Farid used to absorb her pain and her dreams, so that with him she was without either pain or dreams. With him, Fouada was someone else. Fouada without a past or a future, Fouada who lived for the moment, while Farid became her every moment.

How had be become her every moment? How had a man become her whole life? How could a person consume all her attention? She didn't know how it had happened. She wasn't the sort of woman that gives her life away to anyone. Her life

74

was too important to give to one man. Above all, her life was not her own but belonged to the world, which she wanted to change.

She looked around anxiously. Her life belonged to the world, which she wanted to change. She saw people hurrying around, cars speeding about, everything in the world running without stopping. She alone had stopped and her stopping meant nothing to that pushing, rushing movement. What did her stopping mean? What could a drop in the ocean do? Was she a drop in the ocean? Was she a drop? Yes, she was and here was the ocean around her, its waves thrashing and wrestling and racing each other. Could a drop defeat a wave? Could a drop change an ocean? Why was she living this illusion?

She caught her breath and shrank into her coat, walking engrossed in thoughts with head bowed until she arrived home. She went in and threw herself down on the bed fully dressed.

*   *   *

She opened her eyes and looked at her watch. It was seven. She stretched her legs under the cover, feeling pain in her joints. She closed her eyes to go back to sleep, but could not. She had slept continuously for four hours, something she never did during the day. Then she remembered that it had not been continuous, she had awoken once at five o'clock. She hadn't forgotten the meeting with Saati at six, but had closed her eyes, telling herself that she still had another hour. She woke again at a quarter to six and moved her arms to lift the covers and get up, but instead had pulled them up over her head whispering to herself: 'What will happen if I'm a little late?' The next time she opened her eyes it was seven o'clock.

She stayed under the covers stretching, picturing Saati with his huge body and thin legs standing at the door of the laboratory, pressing the bell and getting no answer. She was pleased that sleep had rid her of Saati for ever.

These feelings filled her with energy. The ache in her limbs disappeared, she got up, dressed and went out. As she was going downstairs, she saw her mother open the peep window in the door. Her pale face, criss-crossed with lines behind the narrow iron bars, looked like the creased and crumpled page of a book.

Fouada heard her weak voice saying:

'Are you going to the laboratory?'

'Yes,' she replied.

'Will you be late?'

'I don't know,' she replied distractedly. She wanted to ask her something but instead looked at her in silence, then descended the stairs and went out into the street.

The air was cold and dense but the darkness of the night was even denser. She walked along the street slowly and carefully as if about to collide with something, as if parts of the darkness had solidified, become obstacles she might walk into. She quickened her pace to get out of the dark streets and walk beside the flower garden, inhaling the scent of jasmine. Her heart faltered. Why did she still sense his smell? Why did she still feel his lips on her neck? Why did she still taste his kiss in her mouth? Why did these things remain with her whilst he himself had disappeared? Disappeared – flesh, bones, smell, lips, everything about him. So why did anything – did these tangible memories of him – why did they remain?

But, did they remain? Wasn't this smell her own smell, this touch that of her own skin, this taste her saliva? Why did what was him and what was herself seem entangled and mingled? Was it possible that he was a part of her? Or that she was a part of him? She felt her head and limbs. Which part could it be? She felt her shoulders, chest, stomach. Suddenly she was aware of being in a broad, well-lit street and that many glances were on her. She hurried to the bus stop.

She took the bus to Tahrir Square and walked towards Qasr al-Nil Street. She saw the building in the distance and felt a hard lump move in her heart. The laboratory too had become something oppressive, those empty test tubes, waiting, with mouths open to the air and their transparent glass walls revealing emptiness, ranged in their wooden rack, flaunting their meaningless existence.

She opened the laboratory door and went in. On the floor

was a piece of paper. She picked it up and read the reproachful words: 'I came by at six and did not find you. I'll drop by at nine. Saati.' She looked at the clock. It was half past eight. Just as she was making for the door, she heard the bell, hesitated and stood for a moment behind the door without opening it. The bell rang again and she called out: 'Who is it?' The caretaker's voice reached her and she took a deep breath and opened the door. With the caretaker were a man and a woman.

'They were asking for an analysis laboratory so I brought them here,' she heard the caretaker say.

She led them into the waiting-room where they sat down. In the research room, she put on the white overall, then went out to them.

'We've come for an analysis to see why my wife's sterile,' the man said curtly.

He pointed to the woman who was sitting, head bowed, in silence.

'Have you been to the doctor?' Fouada asked the woman. The woman stared at her in silence and the man replied:

'I've taken her to many doctors. She's had analyses and X-rays but we still don't know what the cause is.'

'Have you also been examined?' Fouada asked him.

The man looked at her in astonishment.

'Me?' he snapped.

'Yes, you,' she replied quietly. 'The man can sometimes be the cause.'

The man got to his feet, pulled his wife up by her arm and shouted:

'What's all this rubbish! She's not going to be analysed here!'

He might have taken his wife and left, but the woman did not move. She stood, staring at her husband, wide-eyed and unblinking, as if she had died and frozen into that position. Nervously, Fouada went over to the woman and tapped her on the shoulder saying:

'Go with your husband, madame.'

As if there were an electrical charge in the touch, the woman started and clung to Fouada's arm with all her strength, crying in a strangled voice:

'I won't go with him! Help me! He beats me every day and takes me to doctors who put metal prongs in my body. They've examined everything, they've analysed everything and said I'm not sterile. It's him that's sick! Him that's sterile! They married me to him ten years ago and I'm still a virgin. He's not a man! In the dark, he doesn't know my backside from my head!'

The man pounced like a wild beast, hitting out at her with his hands, feet and head. The woman hit back. Fouada moved away from them in fear, muttering to herself:

'He's mad! He'll kill the woman in my laboratory! What shall I do?'

She rushed to the door and went out into the corridor to call someone. Suddenly, the door of the lift opened and out came Saati.

In panic, she said:

'A man's beating a woman in there.' At that moment, a piercing scream rang out and Saati rushed into the laboratory. The woman was on the ground with the man kicking her. Saati grabbed hold of him with one hand, slapped him across the face a number of times with the other, then threw him and the woman outside the room and slammed the door.

Fouada stood motionless, listening to their raised voices as they fought with each other on the stairs. She went to the door to see what the man was doing to the woman, but their voices had stopped and the corridor was quiet. She went to the window to watch them leave the building, thinking that the woman would not leave on her own feet, but was astonished to see the man come out followed by the woman walking quietly and with head bowed, as quiet as she had been before the incident. Fouada kept staring at her until she disappeared from view, then left the window and sank into a chair engrossed in thought.

Saati had been watching her, and when she sat down, he also sat on a chair near her.

'You seem upset for the woman,' he said smiling.

She sighed and said:

'She's wretched.'

The prominent eyes flickered as he said:

'No more wretched than others you will see here in your laboratory, but you can't do anything for them.'

He pointed upwards and said:

'They have a god!'

'Is there a god that takes people's mistakes away from them?' she replied irritably.

She didn't know why she uttered the sentence for it was not her own. It was Farid's sentence, she had often heard it from him. The sentence reminded her of Farid and her heart sank. She bowed her head, silent and dejected. She heard Saati say:

'You seem to have been upset by the woman.'

She remained silent. He got up and took a few steps towards her, then said:

'You are kind to everyone . . .'

He paused for a moment, then went on in an agitated voice:

'. . . except me.'

She looked up at him in surprise. He gave an embarrassed smile and said:

'Why did you miss our appointment? Were you busy? Or is this the way all women are?'

The words 'all women' rang in her ear.

'I am not like all women!' she retorted.

'I know you're not like all women,' he said apologetically. 'I know that very well, maybe only too well!'

She opened her mouth to ask him how he knew, but then closed her lips. A long period of silence passed, then she found herself saying:

'What was the matter of importance?'

Sitting down, he said:

'Yesterday, I ran into the under-secretary of the chemistry ministry at a supper party. He's been a friend for many years and I remembered that you work at the chemistry ministry so I mentioned you to him.'

'He doesn't know me,' she said.

Smiling, he said:

'He knows you very well. He described you to me in detail.'

'That's strange,' she exclaimed.

'It would be strange if he didn't know you!' he said.

'Why?' she asked.

'Because he's a man who appreciates beauty!'

She glowered at him angrily and said:

'Is that the important matter?'

'No,' he replied, 'only when I asked him about you, he told me that you were an excellent employee and have excellent reports.'

She smiled sceptically and he said:

'When he talked about you so enthusiastically, I had an idea. I need a chemical researcher in the Board.'

'What do you mean?' she said.

'I mean that I can transfer you to my place, in the Board.'

'To your place?'

'There won't be as much work as in the Ministry,' he went on. 'In fact, you won't have to do anything at all. The Board doesn't have a chemical laboratory.'

She looked at him in astonishment and said:

'Then why should I go?'

He smiled. 'To be in my office.'

She jumped to her feet, her head reeling. She glared steadily into his fish-flickering eyes and said:

'I'm not like that, Mr Saati! I want to work! I want to carry out chemical research! I'd give my life in order to work as a researcher!'

She fell silent for a moment, swallowed hard and then said:

'I hate the Ministry! Loathe it, because I do nothing there. I don't know how my reports can be excellent since I haven't done anything for six years! I won't go to the Board. I won't go to the Ministry, I'll hand in my notice and devote myself exclusively to my laboratory.'

His eyes clouded and he looked down. There was a long silence. Fouada got up, went over to the window then came back and sat on the edge of the chair as if about to get up again. He gazed at her fixedly from behind his thick glasses, a small muscle twitching under his right eye.

'I don't understand you at these moments when you are angry,' he said softly. 'Your eyes are full of buried sadness. Deep inside you there's a pain, I don't know why. You're too young to be so bitter, but it seems you've gone through harsh experiences in your life. But, Fouada, life shouldn't be so serious. Why don't you take life as it comes.'

He went over to where she was sitting and, feeling his soft, fat hand on her shoulder, she jumped to her feet and walked over to the window. He followed her, saying:

'Why waste your youth with such cares. Look . . .' he said, pointing to the streets, 'look how young people like you enjoy life, while you, you are here in your laboratory submerged in analytical work and research. What is it you're searching for? What is it you want that can't be found in that world down there?'

She looked down at the street. The lights, the people, the cars glittered and rippled with an animated, living movement, but the movement was far away from her, separate from her, like a moving picture on a cinema screen, describing a life other than hers, a story other than hers, characters other than hers. She was alone, isolated, constricted within a circle that often threatened to crush her body.

As if from far away she heard Saati's voice.

'You seem tired,' he was saying. 'Take off that white overall and let's go out for some air.'

'I've got a meeting tonight at the policy council,' he continued, looking at his watch, 'but I won't go. These policy meetings are very boring. So much talk and the same talk every time.'

She suddenly remembered the many newspaper articles and pictures of him.

'Apparently you have extensive political activity.'

'Why do you say that?' he asked.

'I seem to have read a lot about it.'

He laughed briefly, his thick glasses reflecting the light, and said:

'Do you believe what you read in the newspapers? I thought that people no longer believe anything that's written. They simply read the papers out of habit, that's all. Do you read the papers every day?'

'I read them and don't read them,' she replied.

He smiled, his teeth showing as yellow as ever.

'What do you really read?' he asked.

Sighing, she replied:

'Chemistry.'

'You talk about chemistry as though you were talking about a man you love. Have you ever been in love?'

As if cold water had been dashed in her face, she recollected that she was standing at the window with Saati beside her, the laboratory empty and silent. She looked at the clock. It was eleven. How had that happened? Hadn't she tried to leave the laboratory before he came? Then she remembered the incident with the man and the woman. But couldn't she have left the laboratory immediately after? She glanced at Saati. His portly body was leaning against the window supported by legs that were thin, like those of a large bird. His eyes – now like a frog's, she thought – darted behind the thick glasses. It seemed to her that before her was a strange type of unknown terrestrial reptile – that might be dangerous. She looked around in consternation and, taking off her white overall, went towards the door, saying:

'I've got to go home immediately.'

He looked surprised, then said:

'We were talking quietly. What happened? Did my question upset you?'

'No, no,' she said. 'Nothing upset me, but my mother's alone at home and I've got to get back immediately.'

Walking with her to the door, he said:

'I can give you a lift in my car.'

She opened the door saying:

'Thank you, but I'll take the bus.'

'The bus? At this time of night? Impossible!'

They went down to the ground floor. He walked ahead of her to the long, blue car and opened the door for her. She saw the caretaker leap to his feet respectfully. She hesitated for a moment, wanting to run away, but unable to. The car door was open and the two men were waiting for her to get in. She got in and Saati closed the door. Then he hurried to the other side of the car, opened the door, got in and started the engine.

The street was practically deserted except for a few people and cars. The air was cold and damp. She saw a man standing in front of a cigarette kiosk. Trembling suddenly, she was about to shout 'Farid!' when the man turned and she caught sight of his face. It was not Farid. She shrank into her coat, shivering with sudden cold. Saati glanced at her and said:

'Someone you know?'

'No,' she said faintly.

'Where do you live?' he asked.

'In Doqi . . .' she replied and gave him the street and house number.

The car crossed Qasr al-Nil Bridge. She saw the Cairo Tower standing erect in the dark like some huge alien creature, its flickering red eyes spinning round and round in its head. Watching the flickering balls circling around she felt dizzy and saw a double tower, with two revolving heads. She rubbed her eyes and the second tower vanished, leaving only one with one spinning head. Then the second one reappeared. Again she rubbed her eyes to make it disappear, but it remained. From the corner of her eyes, she glanced at Saati and saw him with two heads. She trembled and hid her face in her hands.

'You're tired,' she heard his voice say.

Raising her head, she replied:

'I have a headache.'

She looked out of the window. The darkness was intense and all she could see now was a mass of blackness. Suddenly, there came into her mind something she had read about a man who used to chase women, take them to a dark and remote place and murder them. She glanced furtively at Saati – his bulging eyes fixed ahead, his thick and fleshy neck resting on the back of the seat, his thin, pointed knees . . . When he turned towards her, she looked out of the window. The houses were dark and shuttered. No light appeared in the windows, nobody walked in the street.

Why had she got into the car with him? Who was he? She didn't know him, knew nothing about him. Was she awake or having a bad dream? She dug her nails into her thighs to make sure she was there.

The car seemed to have stopped. She trembled and edged over to the door. She heard Saati's voice say:

'Is this the house?'

Looking out of the window, she saw her house and exclaimed in relief:

'Yes, that's it!'

She opened the car door and jumped out. He also got out and walked to the front door with her. The staircase was dark.

'You're tired,' he said to her, 'and the stairs are dark. Shall I see you to the door of your apartment?'

'No, no, thank you,' she replied quickly. 'I'll go up by myself.'

He held out a podgy hand, saying:

'Shall I see you tomorrow?'

'I don't know, don't know,' she replied agitated. 'I might not go out tomorrow.'

His eyes glinted in the dark and he said:

'You're tired. I'll phone you tomorrow.' Smiling, he went on:

'Don't wear yourself out with chemical research!'

She climbed the stairs, her legs quaking, imagining that he was coming up after her. Many crimes happened on darkened staircases. She reached the door of the apartment panting, took out her key, her fingers shaking as she searched for the key hole. She opened the door, went in and quickly closed it behind her. She heard her mother's regular breathing and felt calmer, but she still shivered with cold. She put on some thick wool clothes and tucked herself into bed, her teeth chattering. Then she closed her eyes and lost consciousness.

*　　*　　*

84

In the morning, she awoke to hear her mother's voice saying
something but what it was she didn't know. She saw her mother's
eyes looking down at her anxiously and tried to lift her head from
the pillow . . . it was too heavy . . . inside it something solid
pressed and crushed against the bones of her skull, reverberating,
like the sound of a machine, of clanging metal. She looked around
the room, saw the wardrobe, the window, the clothes-stand, and
the telephone on the shelf. She opened her mouth to speak but
was silenced by a sharp pain in her throat. Her mother's lined
face drew closer and she heard her say:

'Do you want the telephone?'

She shook her head.

'No, no,' she said hoarsely. 'Take it away, into the living-
room. I don't want it here.'

Her mother picked up the phone and held it to her chest as
if it were a dead, black cat. Fouada heard her go into the living-
room, then return.

She buried her head under the covers, hearing her mother
say:

'I heard you coughing in the night. Have you caught a cold?'

From under the covers, she replied:

'It seems like it, mama.'

She moved her parched tongue in her mouth and felt a bitter
taste slip down into her stomach. She wanted to spit it out and
pulled a handkerchief from under the pillow, coughed and tried
to clear her blocked nose. Something hard, like a pebble,
scratched her throat; she sneezed and coughed but the pebble
would not be dislodged. With each breath, it settled further down
inside her chest.

Her mother said something and she replied 'yes' without
knowing what it was and heard the feet shuffle out of the room.
She made a small gap between the bed and the covers to let in
air, but that let in a narrow shaft of light as well and she saw her
hand under her head, a watch around the wrist. She glimpsed
the figure the small hand pointed to and remembered the
Ministry. She closed up the gap and night returned.

Yes, let the night return and stay. Let the light around her dim and let there never be day. What use was day, that endless cycle from home to the Ministry, from the Ministry to the laboratory and from the laboratory to home? What was the point of it all? What was the point of going around in circles? Of moving the muscles of the arms and legs? Of activating the digestion and blood circulation? She remembered Saati saying: 'What are you searching for? What is it you want that can't be found in this world?' She didn't want anything from this world, wanted nothing from it, not even money. What would she do with it anyway? What did a woman do with money in this world? Buy expensive dresses? But of what use were expensive dresses? She didn't remember one of her dresses, didn't remember Farid looking even once at them. She had never felt that her clothes had a value except to cover parts of her body.

And what beside dresses? What did a woman do with money in this world other than buy dresses? Buy jewellery and face powder? That white powder with which women cover their faces, to hide those blood vessels that run through living skin? What is left of living skin after its blood colour is blotted out? Only dull, dead skin, chalky white, etiolated.

What else besides powder and dresses and jewels? What did a woman want from the world? Going to the cinema? Visiting women friends? Gossip and jealousy and the pursuit of marriage?

But she didn't want any of these. She didn't buy make-up, didn't go to the cinema, had no women friends and did not pursue marriage. So what was she seeking?

She pressed her head into the pillow and clenched her teeth in frustration. What do I want? What do I want? Why don't I want those things that other women want? Aren't I a woman like them?

Lifting the cover from her face a little she saw her slender fingers and nails, just like her mother's. She touched her skin and body, the skin and body of her mother. She really was a woman, so why didn't she want what other women wanted. Why?

Yes, why, why? She didn't know. Was chemistry the reason? But was she the only woman to have studied chemistry? Was

86

Madame Curie the reason? But was she the only woman to have heard of Madame Curie? Was it the chemistry teacher? But where was the chemistry teacher? She knew nothing about her, had heard nothing of her since leaving school. Did her life depend on a word spoken by some obscure woman? Was it her mother? But did her mother know anything about the wide world outside the four walls of the house? Was it Farid? But where was Farid? Who was he? She didn't know anyone who knew him, didn't know where he was, didn't know even if he had ever really existed. Maybe he was an illusion, a dream? He was absent and as long as he was absent, how could she distinguish dream from reality? If he had only left a note in his handwriting she could have been sure. Yes, with a piece of paper, she would have known, whilst with her head, arms and legs, she could know nothing. Neither her body nor her head could know anything. Everything inside her head had been reduced to a meaningless, muffled clangour. Everything inside her had been catalysed into a dull, continuous hum, like that perceived when everything is silent.

Yes, there was complete silence deep within that body outstretched and incapacitated beneath the covers, silence and only silence. It was incapable of saying anything. The words that came out of its lips were not its own words but simply the random echoes of words heard before; the words of others, words that Farid, her mother, the chemistry teacher had spoken, or words she had read in a book. Yes, it repeated only what it had heard and read and, like a wall, could only voice echoes.

Her body under the covers was heavy and inert – like a stone – she was hot and sweated profusely. A warm, viscous substance poured from her nose. She pulled a handkerchief from under the pillow and blew her nose hard. It dripped like a worn-out tap. She was not a clean, dry wall, but an oozing, dripping wall – with a noxious, involuntary wetness.

She kicked the cover from her body, wanting to kick off her arms, legs and whole body, but it adhered, clung to her, remained attached to her, lying on top of her – an oppressive weight and obscene wetness, like the body of another person, a stranger.

A stranger, with all the strangeness of some person she might

87

encounter in the street, the strangeness of the caretaker, of Saati. She shuddered. Yes, an utter stranger who swallowed food, not knowing what happened to it. Sometimes she heard a noise in her stomach, like the mewing of a cat, as if she didn't know what was happening there, where all that quantity of food went. Like a mill, it turned and turned and pulverized solid things. There was only that turning and the pulverizing and nothing else. Nothing else.

What else could there be? That illusion which beckoned through the mist? Test tubes from whose mouths a new gas danced? What could a new gas do? A new hydrogen bomb? A rocket with a new nuclear head? What did the world lack? A new means of killing?

Why the killing? Was there nothing else of use? Something to eliminate hunger? Disease? Suffering? Oppression? Exploitation? Yes, yes, here was the wall, echoing words it had heard from Farid. What do you know about hunger? About disease? What do you know about suffering or oppression? What about exploitation? What do you know about them and about that which you talk of to people whilst not even living with people? You look at them from a distance, study their movements and houses as if they were moving images on a blank screen. Have you ever been hungry? Have you ever seen a hungry person? That woman begging on the pavement of the Ministry, a young child in her lap, did you even see her? Did you look into her eyes? Wasn't it only her sun-beaten back you saw and didn't you envy her?

Do you know anything of this? Why then persist in this illusion? Don't you eat and drink and urinate and sleep like others? Why aren't you like others? Why?

Yes, why, why? Why aren't you like others, calmly accepting life as it is? Why not take life as it comes? Even these words are not yours. Didn't you hear this very same question from Saati yesterday in the laboratory? Do you store up all the words inside you? Even Saati's words? How stupid you are! Can't you say one word of your own?

Fouada awoke to the sound of her mother's voice. She saw

her standing beside her, holding a glass of tea in her thin, veined hand. She stared at her long, slender, wrinkled fingers. Her own were as long and slender as her mother's and would become as wrinkled as hers with gnarled joints, like dry twigs. She looked up and saw her lined face, her dry lips parted, the same gap, the same teeth. Let the same lines cover her face too. Let her own legs become incapable of moving quickly, and her feet shuffle like hers.

She reached out weakly and took the glass of tea. Her mother sat on the edge of the bed looking at her. Why was she silent? Why didn't she say anything? Why didn't she raise her hand to the sky and repeat her old supplication? But the dream was gone, the illusion lost. She had not given birth to a natural wonder. Who had told her that she would? Why her in particular? Why her womb in particular? Millions of wombs gave birth every day so what had put this illusion in her head? Maybe she had inherited the illusion from her own mother, just as Fouada had inherited it from her. Some woman in the family must have imagined her womb to be different, must have begun it all. Someone had begun it, there always had to be someone.

She heard her mother say:

'What's wrong, Fouada? Why don't you speak?'

Her voice was so sad she wanted to cry, but she held back the tears and opened her mouth to say:

'I've got a bad headache.'

'Shall I get you an aspirin?' her mother asked.

'Yes,' she nodded.

As her mother went back into the living-room the telephone rang. Fouada jumped out of bed, shaking. Was it Saati? She stood in the doorway looking at the phone. Her mother went over to answer it, but she shouted:

'Don't answer it, mama! There's someone I don't want to talk to . . .'

But then, suddenly, she thought it might be Farid and rushed to the telephone. She lifted the receiver and gasped: 'Hello.' The oily voice of Saati came to her and she slumped into a chair, flaccid and lifeless.

Part Three

Fouada left the Ministry and walked alongside the rusty iron railings. Her head was heavy and her heart convulsed, inside it that hard, perpetual lump. She saw the woman sitting on the pavement, holding her child to her chest, empty hand reaching out. The street was noisy and crowded but no one noticed the outstretched arm. One pushed her aside to clear his path, another trod on her in his hurry. She heard the child crying as she passed by and saw that small skeleton with sunken eyes, prominent cheeks and a small pouting mouth trying in vain to suck a piece of brown wrinkled skin that hung from the woman's chest.

She put her hand in her pocket to take out a piastre, but kept it inside her pocket. She raised her eyes to the street. Long cars followed one after the other, within each a shiny head that reflected the light and a fleshy neck that resembled Saati's.

She took out the piastre and held it in her hand for a moment. What good was a piastre? Would it clothe the bones of that small skeleton in flesh? Would it cause the milk to flow from that shrivelled flap of skin? She chewed her lips. What could she do? A chemical discovery to eliminate hunger? A new gas for millions to breathe instead of food?

She let the piastre fall from her fingers into the empty open palm. A piastre would do nothing, but let it be a passing charity, to ease her conscience, a trifling price to pay and forget.

Here were Farid's words again. His voice in her head had a sting. Her eyes searched for his brown, shining ones. There were many eyes around, so why his in particular? When she gazed, close, into his eyes she did not feel the astonishment she felt when looking closely into other eyes, even her mother's or into her own. When she stared at her eyes in the mirror, their familiar shape disappeared, as if they were the eyes of an unknown animal. But Farid's eyes had something strange in them, strange yet familiar, that grew more and more familiar and was not at all strange. When the distance between the two of them vanished and they touched, she felt utterly secure.

Was all that an illusion? Had her feelings so betrayed her? If her feelings lied, in what could she believe? Words of ink on paper? An official document with the Ministry seal on it? A certificate printed in duplicate? What could she believe if her feelings lied?

She stopped abruptly to ask: But what are feelings? Could she touch them? Could she see them? Could she smell them? Could she put them in a test tube and analyse them? Feelings, mere feelings, an invisible movement in her head, like illusions, like dreams, like some hidden force. Could her scientific mind believe in such nonsense?

She looked around, confused. Were feelings true or false? Why, when she looked into Farid's eyes, did she feel that he was familiar and when she looked into Saati's eyes, feel that he was a thief? Was that illusion or knowledge? Was it a random movement in the optic nerve or a conscious movement in the brain cells? How could she distinguish between the two? How could she distinguish the mistaken vibration of a pressed nerve from the healthy idea emanating from a brain cell? And how did a brain cell think? How could a small mass of protoplasm think? Where did an idea come from and how did it pass through her cellular tissue? Electrically? A chemical reaction?

She looked up to see what was around her and noticed the building with the white placard bearing her name in black letters. Her heart shrank. Test tubes with open mouths – empty – a tongue of flame burning the air, burning itself, that insistent whistle echoing in her ear when everything fell silent.

Yes, that was the laboratory. But it wasn't a laboratory any longer. It had become a trap, ensnaring her impotence, ensnaring her ignorance, ensnaring the silence and the nothingness in her head.

She passed the entrance to the building without entering, walked on a few paces, then stopped. Where was she going? Everywhere had become like the laboratory, a trap for impotence, silence and the whistle in her ears. Home and the Ministry, the telephone and the street, everything interlocked, undeviating.

She retraced her steps to the building, to go to her laboratory. There was no way out. The trap opened its jaws and she entered between them. Saati would come in a while. He would surely come, to the laboratory or wherever. He knew her every place: telephone number, house, Ministry and laboratory. He would come in his long blue car, with his bulging eyes and fleshy neck. He would surely come, for why didn't the earth lose its equilibrium, the test-tube rack shake and the empty tubes fall and break? Why did the earth turn so perfectly? Why was its equilibrium not disturbed, just once?

She had entered the laboratory, put on the white overall and now stood at the window watching the street and observing the cars as if waiting for him, for Saati. And she really was waiting for him. She saw the long blue car pull up in front of the building and Saati get out, with his portly body on thin legs.

As she dragged her feet to the door, she noticed her reflection in the long mirror beside it. Her face was thinner and longer, her eyes dulled and sunken into their sockets, the gape of her mouth even wider, her teeth even more prominent, just like her mother's.

She closed her lips to hide her teeth, clamping her jaws together to crush her teeth, or something else, between them. There must be something to crush. She ground her teeth making a metallic sound. When the door bell rang, she made a sharp gesture with her fist and said: 'I won't open it . . .' and held herself quite still, inanimate. Again the bell rang; her breath quickened into a rapid panting. Then, quivering, she opened the door.

*　　*　　*

He was carrying a small packet in his cushiony hand. His upper lip lifted, revealing the large, yellow teeth, and his prominent eyes quivered behind the thick glasses.

'A small present,' he said, putting the package on the table and sitting down.

She remained standing, staring at the thin green ribbon tied around the packet.

'Open it,' she heard him say hoarsely.

He was giving her an order, had taken upon himself the right to give her orders, had paid the price of this right and had the right to use it. She looked at his eyes. They were quieter, as if he had begun to gather confidence in himself. He was giving her something, having paid a price for her, and was now able to buy something from her, anything, even the right to order her to open the packet. She remained on her feet, unmoving.

He got up and opened the package himself. He came over to where she stood, held out a box to her and said:

'What do you think of this?'

She saw something glittering against red velvet.

'I don't understand about these things,' she said distractedly.

He stared at her in surprise and said:

'That's a genuine diamond.'

He brought his face close to her and she saw his fish-like eyes, covered by a dark membrane that hid the natural sparkle.

He had perhaps paid a great deal of money, perhaps a hundred pounds or more, but what was it worth to her?

She had no use for such things, didn't wear rings or bracelets or necklaces. If even the skin that enclosed her body irritated her, how could she wrap other cords around her limbs? If she was aware of the weight of her own muscles and bones, how could she weigh down her limbs with metallic chains, of whatever kind?

He came closer still, repeating:

'The stone's a genuine diamond.'

She smiled in silence. He would never understand. To her a genuine diamond was useless. What was the difference between it and a piece of tin or glass? Does the earth make a distinction between things?

That familiar quivering had returned to his eyes.

'What gift would please you?' he muttered in a defeated voice.

She didn't know what to reply. What presents did Farid give

her? Did Farid even buy her presents? She didn't remember him buying her anything. There was nothing that could be bought. What could he buy? His words? The tone of his voice? The light in his eyes? The warmth of his breath and the sweetness of his lips?

Saati put a soft, plump hand on her shoulder saying:

'What can I give you to make you happy?'

The muscles of her shoulder contracted to shrug off the weight of his hand. She turned around. What could he give her? Could he give her the elusive contents of the test tube? Could he give her that lost idea? Could he stop that uninterrupted and meaningless high-pitched humming in her head? Would she lift the receiver one day, the ringing stop and the voice of one for whom she searched reach her?

She looked at him. He was putting the box into his pocket with unsteady fingers. There was nothing he could do, what could she tell him? She took a few steps, head lowered, then said in a constricted voice:

'Let's go out. I'm nearly choking.'

* * *

The long blue car took them through the streets of Cairo. They remained silent until the car emerged into the countryside near the Pyramids, then she heard him say, almost brusquely:

'There's a secret in your life I don't understand. Why don't you open your heart to me?'

She glanced at him briefly, then fixed her eyes on the expanse of desert and said:

'I don't know if my life has a secret or a meaning. I just eat and sleep like any animal and do nothing useful for anyone.'

He half sighed, half grunted.

'Are you still at that stage?' he asked.

'What do you mean?'

'I went through that stage twenty years ago,' he said. He was silent for a moment, then went on:

'But I found out that real life is something else.'

'What do you mean?' she said.

97

Grimacing, he replied:

'Lofty principles always brought me into conflict with real life. They called me a non-conformist.'

'Who are they?' she asked.

'My colleagues at university.'

'Did you go to university?'

'I was a teacher with principles.'

'And then what happened?' she asked.

He laughed briefly, then said:

'Then I conformed.'

He turned to her, his eyes steady for a moment, and said:

'There was no other way.'

'Did you write any papers when you were at university?' she asked.

'I did seventy-three.'

'Seventy-three?' she exclaimed. 'How? That's impossible!'

Biting his lips, he replied:

'It was very simple. I only put my name to them.'

'And the real researcher?' she asked in dismay.

'He was a young man still trying to make it,' he said.

'But,' she shouted, 'didn't you do even one in-depth study of your own?'

'Impossible,' he said simply. 'Undertaking any real research takes a lifetime and ruins the chances for real life.'

She fell silent for a moment, grave-faced, saying to herself:

'Just as I thought the first time I saw him! The eyes of a thief! He stole seventy-three studies!'

'And then what?' she said.

'Then I became a great professor,' he laughed.

'And then?'

'A person's ambitions are limitless,' he said smiling. 'Then I went into politics.'

'And what do you know about politics?' she said.

'Everything. It's enough to befriend this or that one and to repeat slogans in an educated accent.'

She looked at the fleshy neck in disgust and said:

'And do you respect yourself now?'

'How does one respect oneself, Fouada?' he said in the same tone. 'Self-respect doesn't happen in a vacuum. It comes from the respect of others. And I, I am the head of the Supreme Board for Building and Construction, head of the political council. The newspapers write about me. I talk on the radio and television and give advice to people. The whole world respects me so how can I not respect myself!'

He pulled the car up by the side of the road and looking at her, said:

'Believe me, Fouada, I respect myself, but even more than that, I believe the lies I repeat in front of people. I have grown to believe them from repeating them out loud so often and so convincingly. What is a person, Fouada? What is a person if not a collection of feelings? And what are feelings if not the accumulation of life's experiences? Should I ignore all these experiences and inhabit a realm of principles and theories which cannot be applied to the real world? Should I, for example, do as Hassanain Effendi did?'

He fell silent for a moment as if reviving old memories, then continued:

'Hassanain Effendi was a colleague of mine at university. He believed that he had a new idea in his head and began a scientific study. He would buy test tubes out of his meagre wages, went all over to gather equipment, and then what happened?'

'What did happen?' she asked in concern.

He sucked his lips and said:

'His colleagues got in before him and registered superficial studies in order to get promotion while the senior professors were enraged with him for refusing to sell his name to anyone. Then they dismissed him on a trumped-up charge.'

'Impossible!' she exclaimed, shaking her head.

'I ran into him in the street a few months ago,' he said quietly. 'He stared ahead, looking dazed, and didn't recognize me. He was smiling, showing his yellow teeth, and his toes stuck out of his shoes. It was all very painful. Does anyone respect Hassanain Effendi?'

'I respect him,' she shouted.

'And who are you?' he said very softly.

'Me? Me?' she said angrily.

She felt her voice fading and that she was choking. She opened the car door and walked out into the desert. Saati got out after her and she heard him say:

'The truth is bitter, Fouada, but you must know it. I could lie to you, nothing would be easier. I'm used to it and practised at it, but I love you, Fouada, and want to spare you confusion and distress.'

He took her delicate, slender hand in his soft, fleshy one and whispered:

'I love you!'

She pulled her hand away and shouted angrily:

'Leave me alone! I don't want to hear a word!'

He left her and went back to the car. She walked alone in the desert and the humming began in her ear. Yes, let the humming go on. Silence was better than that sound. Let the meaningless, uninterrupted clamour fill her head, for it was better than those words. And you, Farid, you continue to be absent. What would you do if you were here? What would you do? What does a drop in the ocean do? What can a drop in the ocean do?

She spread her arms in the air and embraced the void. Yes, the void was better, nothingness was better. But how to become nothing? Her feet moved over the sand, her breath entered and left her lungs, the beats of her heart were still in her ears.

How could her body disappear? She stamped on the ground. Why can't I disappear? She held her breath to stop the air going in and out – pressed her hand to her heart to stop it beating.

It seemed to her that the air had stopped coming in, that her chest no longer rose and fell, and that she could no longer hear her heartbeats. She smiled. She had disappeared. But there was something heavy lying on her chest, something bitter burned her throat. A strange nauseous smell filled her nostrils and a soft, fleshy hand held hers. She tried to pull it away but could not find it. It had disappeared.

*　　*　　*

100

She opened her eyes and saw the wardrobe, the clothes-stand, the window and the ceiling with that jagged patch, and looked around bewildered. So she had not disappeared? This was her very same room, this her heavy head on the pillow and her body with its weight and density stretched out under the covers. This was the sound of shuffling feet approaching the room and this the brown, lined face looking in from the door. She saw the large eyes looking at her and heard the feeble voice say:

'What's the matter, daughter? What's the matter, Fouada?'

She shook her head, saying hoarsely:

'Nothing, mama, if only I were dead!'

'Why, Fouada? Death is for old people like me. You used to hate even the mention of it.'

'Farid,' she whispered.

'What?' her mother exclaimed in alarm. 'Is Farid dead?'

'No, no! He's only away, he'll come back,' she said shuddering.

She hid her face under the cover, swallowing the strangely bitter and acrid taste in her mouth. Where had it come from? She began to remember. She had been standing in the desert staring into space, had felt Saati behind her. He had put his arm around her waist and his eyes came nearer, growing larger and more prominent. She had felt his cold lips press on her lips, and his large teeth against hers. Her nostrils filled with a strange metallic smell like that of rusted iron, and her mouth filled with bitter saliva.

Yes, she saw and felt, but not clearly, not surely. It was all slow-moving and distant – like a nightmare. She had tried to hit him but her arm would not lift.

She reached beneath the cover and felt her arm. It was there and she moved it to pull the handkerchief from under the pillow and spat into it repeatedly. But the hot bitterness clung inside her mouth and she felt she was about to vomit. She threw back the covers and went to the bathroom, but the desire to vomit had passed. Almost viciously she scrubbed her teeth with brush and paste, and gargled, but the bitterness burned in her throat and was slowly seeping down.

Her mother's slender hand was on her shoulder.

'What happened to Farid?'

She raised her eyes. There was a strange look in her mother's eyes and she shuddered.

'I don't know. I don't know. Leave me alone, mama.'

She returned to her room and sat on the edge of the bed, clutching her head in her hands. The telephone rang and she jumped. It must be him. His mean, coarse voice would come down the line. He would surely come. Why didn't the earth spin off balance and the telephone crash and break? But the earth turned without fail, and the telephone would neither crash nor break. His voice would surely come through the holes in the receiver just as the wind comes through holes in the door. He would come without fail. His bitterness would burn her throat and his nauseous smell fill her nostrils. Why not dress and run away?

She hauled up her heavy body and dressed. Her mother's eyes watched her in silence, a strange expression in them. Stumbling to the door she paused to look at her. . . . She could stay with her – wanted to stay with her – but she opened the door and went out.

Mindlessly she dragged her body through the streets. Her head was quiet, but not calmly, naturally quiet, but with a kind of paralysis, tranquillized, as if her brain cells were stilled by drugs.

She let her feet go their own way without directions from the head. Why always the head? Why wasn't the mind in the legs? The head does nothing more than be carried on the shoulders, then it rules and controls, while the legs do the work as well as carry the head, the shoulders and the whole body without ever being in control. Just as in life. Those who work and toil do not rule while the heads continue to be carried by necks, relishing the fruits and issuing controls.

Farid's words again. The tone of his voice, the movement of his hand, were still in her head. Why? When he was gone? How did his words, his movements come to be creeping through her head once again?

She walked beside the flower garden. The scent of jasmine drifted to her. Farid's breath on her face with its smell, its warmth, and the touch of his lips on her neck returned. Her pale hand lifted – to touch his face – but it trembled in the air, then fell by her side.

The Nile was just as it always was, languid, eternal and infinite; its long, ruffled body, winding, languorous – like an aged whore, abandoned, content and without care. Fouada looked about her. Everything was abandoned, content, without care. And she? Couldn't she too be without care – carefree? Couldn't she become one of those mummified heads in the office? Couldn't she put her name to research she had not done like the smart, successful ones do?

Her eyes scanned the sky and earth. What had she wanted from the start? She hadn't wanted anything, hadn't wanted to succeed or shine. She had only felt, felt there was something in her that was not in others. She would not simply live and die, and the world remain the same. She had felt something in her head, the conception of a unique idea, but how to give it birth? The idea was awake, alive and struggling, but it did not emerge, seeming as if imprisoned by a thick wall, thicker than the bones of her skull.

She was all feelings, but how else does anything new begin? How did any discoverer who changed science or history begin? Doesn't it all begin with feelings? And what are feelings? An obscure idea, a mysterious movement in the brain cells. Yes. Isn't the beginning always a mysterious movement in the brain cells? So why mock at her feelings? Why deny them? The first time she saw Saati, hadn't she felt that he was a thief? Had her feelings about the towering building and the long car betrayed her? Had the Supreme Board and the political council and the newspaper articles changed her first feelings? Despite everything, hadn't she continued to feel that he was a thief? Hadn't her brain cells picked up that invisible lie in the shiftiness of his bulging eyes? So why disregard her feelings?

She stood still for a moment and asked herself had she ever before doubted her feelings? When had the doubt begun? When?

She glanced around and caught sight of the door of the small restaurant and remembered. It was that night, that dark, gusty night when she entered the restaurant and saw the empty, uncovered table, the wind hitting it from all sides, like the buffeted stump of a tree.

Her feet approached the restaurant door apprehensively. Should she go in? What would she find? Perhaps, perhaps she would find him, perhaps he had come back. Her feet moved slowly, step by step towards the door. She paused to take a deep breath, then entered the long tree-lined passageway, knees quaking and heart pounding. She would come out of the passageway and look at the table and not find him. Better to go back right now. Yes, better to go back . . . yet there was a hope that he was there, sitting at the table, his back leaning slightly forward, his thick black hair, his ears always flushed, his gleaming brown eyes in which that strange thing moved, that thing she sensed without seeing, something which made him *him*, his individuality, his particular words, thoughts and smell, made him Farid and not one of a million other men.

She turned to go back, but her feet moved her forward, down to the end of the passageway, then turned to the left. She stood with head bowed for a moment, unable to look up. Then she raised her head and her eyes met a brick wall. The table, everything, had gone, all she saw was a short wall in the open-air like those walls that are built around the dead.

She heard a soft voice behind her ask:

'Do you want any fish?'

She turned to see a woman carrying a child. It was not a child, more a tiny skeleton, its small toothless jaws grasping a shrivelled breast that hung from the woman's chest like a strip of leather. The woman looked at her through half-closed, congested eyes and repeated in a weak voice:

'Do you want any fish?'

Fouada swallowed the bitterness in her mouth and said absently:

'There used to be a small restaurant here.'

'Yes,' the woman replied, 'but the owner lost his money and left the place.'

'And who took it?' she asked.

'The municipality,' the woman said.

'Who built this wall?'

'The municipality,' the woman replied.

Contemplating the wide open space, she asked:

'What did they build it for?'

Tugging at a dry breast and putting it between the child's jaws, the woman answered:

'My husband says the municipality built this wall to put its name on.'

The woman added:

'Do you want any fish?'

She smiled weakly and said:

'Not today. Perhaps I'll come back to buy another time.'

She left by the small door and walked down the street. There was no longer hope, no longer anything, only a brick wall, a short brick wall, good for nothing except the names of the dead.

No, there was only a wall. Was there nothing else? There was nothing. Everything had disappeared, as when a dream fades. What was the difference between dream and reality? If he had left a small note in his handwriting she could have known, a piece of paper with letters on it could have made the difference between dream and reality, whereas she, with her head and arms and legs, she could not.

She shook her head angrily. It was as heavy as stone, as if it too had become a wall. Was there anything else? Anything apart from a blank wall that returned an echo, returned what it heard and what it read? Could it say anything of its own? Had it ever said anything new . . . that no one had ever said before? Did it not emit that uninterrupted, humming sound when all was silent?

The humming began in her head. Holding her head in her hands she sat on a stone wall. She stayed with head lowered for a second, then raised her weary eyes to the sky. Was it all a dream? Were her feelings an illusion? If her feelings lied, what was true? What could she believe? A name written on a wall? A name signed to a study? A word printed in a newspaper?

The sky . . . was it the highest wall of all? Silent like any other wall? Raising her hands in the air she said out loud:

'Are you a wall? Why are you silent?'

A man walking in the street stared at her and approached, examined her with narrow, black eyes, then smiled a half-smile and said:

'I'll pay you only one riyal. Your legs are too thin.'

She looked at him, alarmed, then dragged her heavy body off the wall and let her legs carry her unthinkingly home.

*   *   *

The door of the house was open, the living-room was full of people. Faces she knew and those she didn't looked at her curiously. She heard a loud sound like a scream and saw a face that resembled her mother's, but unlined. It was her aunt Souad, with her fat body in a tight black dress, who yelled: 'Fouada!'

She wrapped her short, fat arms around her. Many women surrounded her, screaming with one voice, the smell of scent rose from their black clothing. Half choking, she pushed the fat bodies away from her, shouting loudly:

'Get away from me!'

The women withdrew, bewildered. With heavy steps, she went slowly to her mother's room. She was lying on her bed, her head and body covered. Fearfully she approached and cautiously put out a hand to draw back the cover. Her mother's head wrapped in a white headcloth appeared, her face lined, eyes closed, mouth pressed tight, small gold earrings in her ears. She was sleeping as she always did, except that no breathing was perceptible. Fouada searched her face. Her features were changing bit by bit, as though collapsing into her face and clinging to her bones, the blood draining away.

A shiver ran through her body. Her mother's face had become like that of a stone statue, radiating an eerie coldness. She replaced the cover over the head, trembling. The screaming ran in her ears, uninterrupted and piercing. Dazed, she stumbled to her room, but it, too, was filled with faces she did not know. She went into the living-room. Strange eyes surrounded and encircled her. Screams echoed in her head. Without realizing, she walked towards the door, stood behind it for a moment, then rushed down the stairs and ran out into the street.

She didn't know where she was running, but simply ran, looking over her shoulder as if pursued by a ghost. She wanted to escape, to somewhere distant, where no one would see her. But he did not let her escape. He saw her running down the street, stopped the blue car, and ran after her. He caught her arm, saying:

'Fouada, where are you running?'

Gasping, she stopped and saw his eyes bulging, and quivering behind his glasses. In a bewildered voice, she said:

'I don't know.'

'I phoned you an hour ago,' he said, 'and heard the news.'

Lowering his head, he added:

'I came to offer you my condolences.'

She wheeled round, the screams still ringing in her ears, the strange staring eyes crowding her from every direction. Burying her face in her hands she broke into tears. Saati helped her to the car, which took them from street to street. On the horizon the sun's last rays were fading. Across the sky, grey, tear-stained cloud-bodies were spreading. The car emerged into the open country and the desert glowed beneath the headlamps. She remembered her mother's face in the morning, waiting for her before she left the house. There had been a curious look in her eyes, a pleading look asking her to stay, but she had not seen that look as clearly she saw it now. Or had she seen it and consciously or unconsciously pretended not to? She had often pretended to ignore her silent looks, often pretended to ignore them. She had wanted to hurry and get out. Why had she hurried? Why did she go out? Where was she going? Why hadn't she stayed with her this last day? She had been alone, completely alone. Had she called out to her and she was not there to hear? Had she wanted some water and found no one to bring it? Why had she left her this day? Could this day ever return again?

The tears poured into her nose and throat and she opened her mouth for air, gasping, sobbing. The car had stopped. Saati sitting beside her was silent, looking at her long, pale face and staring fixedly into her green, distraught eyes. He put out his plump hand and took her trembling slender one.

'Don't be sad, Fouada. This is how life is. There's no life without death.'

He was silent for a moment, then said:

'What's the use of being sad? It only makes you ill. I'm never sad, or if it happens that I am, I think about happy things or listen to soothing music.'

He put out his hand and turned on the radio. A dance tune came out. The tears froze to a lump in her throat and, feeling she would choke, she opened the door and stepped out into the desert. A light cool breeze tightened her muscles, but her body was heavy. She moved her legs to shake off that oppressive weight but it bore down on her. She opened her mouth to scream, to expel the lump from her throat, but the muscles of her mouth expanded and contracted, expelling nothing. The lump slid into her neck, and its muscles expanded and contracted, then it moved to her chest and stomach; these muscles too began to expand and contract. But like the tentacles of some hydra-headed serpent the lump slithered into her whole body, until all her muscles expanded and contracted in rapid, violent spasms like convulsions. How desperately she wanted to rid her body of that choking, creeping thing

The tune from the car radio rang through the silent desert. Her ears were deaf to it but it filled the air and entered her with every breath. Panting, she wanted to stop, to be still, but her muscles ignored her consciousness and her body began to tremble to the tune, discharging the venom from the pent-up energy and unconsciously revelling in the joy of dancing.

Yes, she had lost conscious control and was abandoned to the delight of the violent movement, yet one small point in her head, perhaps one single brain cell, still retained consciousness. It still knew that she was in the desert, that Saati was standing beside her, that she was extremely sad, that her mother was

dead, Farid was absent, the idea of research was lost, her life in
the Ministry empty.

She shook her head fiercely to separate out that one conscious
cell, but it would not be dislodged. It had taken hold, solidified
and began to rattle around her head, ripping through her languid
brain cells like a pointed pebble.

The music stopped suddenly. Perhaps it had reached the end
or perhaps Saati had turned off the radio. Her body crumpled on
to the sand, breathless and soaked in sweat. When was the last
time her body had been so drenched in sweat? When was the last
time she had danced so wildly, uninhibitedly? Listened to
Theodorakis? When was the last time Kazantzakis had said only
madness destroys? Farid used to fight madness. He used to say
that the madness of one individual means incarceration or death,
whereas the madness of millions . . . What does the madness of
millions mean? Farid? Knowledge and hunger, he used to say.
Hunger exists, only knowledge is lacking. And why don't they
have knowledge, Farid? How can they, Fouada, when everything
around them is either silent or lying?

She opened her eyes. She was lying on the sand beside a
huge bulk with bulging eyes from which emanated something
false and thievish. She heard a hoarse voice say:

'The most wonderful dance I've ever seen and the most
beautiful dancer that exists!'

His arms were around her, filling her nostrils with a rusty
metallic smell and her mouth with bitter, acrid saliva. She saw
his bulbous eyes grow larger and more prominent, a strange
frightening look in them. She struggled to turn, in terror, but saw
only the desert and darkness. She tried to breathe but couldn't
and with all her strength pushed him away from her, leapt up
and ran. He ran after her.

Before her the spreading darkness, behind her that bulbous-
eyed shadow, stalking her. It seemed that the flat desert in front
of her was rising and spinning into two great, bulging eyes as she
ran in a long narrow trench between them. The black convex
bulk of the sky, too, had become great, bulging eyes, towering

over and pressing down on her. She stumbled against something round and solid, fell to the ground and lost consciousness.

Lost consciousness except for that one, conscious cell into which her five senses were polarized. She could still see, hear, feel, taste and smell. She felt a plump, fleshy hand on her chest, smelled a rusty metallic smell, tasted bitter, acrid saliva.

The cushiony hand became coarse, trembling fingers. The trembling did not stay in one place but crept lower, to her stomach and thighs. She saw his thick creased, fleshy neck like the trunk of an old tree out of which jutted small black buds which might have lived and developed but instead had died and decayed. His unbuttoned silk shirt revealed a hairless, fleshy chest, an unfastened leather belt hung around a bloated belly from which hung a pair of thin, hairless legs. His belly rose and fell with his spasmodic breathing and from inside him came a curious, muffled rattle like the groan of a sick animal.

A strange, heavy coldness enveloped her body, a coldness it had known only once before. She had been lying on a leather sheet surrounded by metal instruments – scalpels and syringes and scissors. The doctor picked up a long syringe and jabbed its needle into her arm. That same heavy coldness had coursed through her body as though she were plunged into a bath of ice and her body grew heavier and slowly drowned.

Only now there was no water beneath her but something soft . . . like sand. Cold air entered her dishevelled dress, hot, bitter saliva gathered in her throat, the smell of something old and rusted invaded her nostrils. A panting, shuddering bulk lay beside her, its thin legs limp and shaking. She tried to open her mouth to spit but could not. Her eyelids grew heavy and closed.

*   *   *

She opened her eyes to see daylight streaming through the slats of the shutters. She looked around in bewilderment. Everything in her room was normal, the wardrobe, clothes-stand, window, ceiling and jagged circle. She heard shuffling feet in the living-room, approaching her room. She looked at the door expecting her mother's face to appear, but a long while passed and nothing happened. Remembering, she leaped out of bed on to her feet. Trembling, she went to the living-room and apprehensively approached the door of her mother's room. Was it all a dream? Or was she really dead? She put her head round the door, saw the empty bed and retreated in fear. She went to the kitchen, to the dining-room, to the bathroom but her mother was nowhere. Dizzily she leaned her head against the wall. A solid lump whirled in her skull, knocking against the bones. Bitterness scalded her throat. Supporting herself against the wall, she staggered to the sink and opened her mouth to spit, but the bitterness pressed on her stomach and she vomited. The obscene, rusty smell emanated from her mouth, her nose, her clothes. She undressed, stood beneath the shower and scrubbed her body with a loofa and soap but the smell clung to her flesh. It had entered her pores and cells and into her blood.

Still clutching the walls, she returned to her room. Looking around in distraction, her eyes settled on the face of her mother in the photograph hanging near the wardrobe. Her mother seemed to look out at her with large, jaundiced eyes, feebly pleading with her to stay. She covered the face with her hand. Would her mother never lose that accusing look? Had she not paid for her sin? Wasn't she filled with that burning bitter taste? Wasn't her body steeped in that concentrated smell of old rust? Was there any grief greater than this? What was grief? How did people grieve? A loud scream clearing the voice and relieving pent-up feelings? Black clothing whose newness refreshed the body? Banquets and slaughtered meat stimulating the appetite and filling the stomach? Was there a dead mother who enjoyed more grief than this? Was there another mother whose daughter swallowed poison after her? Was there a mother's death greater than this death? Was there a greater filial repayment?

She went to bed feeling somewhat calmer and stretched out her arms and legs, but the heaviness was still on her body, the bitterness still burned. When, when would this heaviness relent and this burden lift?

The telephone rang. It was him. None other. There was only him left. There was nothing else left but to swallow poison day after day. Her insides would be eroded by the acrid burning, her body saturated by concentration of old, cold rust. Only a slow death remained.

She put out a slender hand and raised the receiver. The hoarse, oily voice came through:

'Good morning, Fouada. How are you?'

'Alive,' she said listlessly.

'What are you doing tonight?' he asked.

'I don't know,' she said. 'I have nothing left.'

'What about me? I am left,' he said.

'Yes,' she said, 'there's only you left.'

'I'll pick you up at the laboratory at half past eight,' he said.

*　　*　　*

Walking out of the door she noticed something, something white and glistening behind the glass panel. She stepped back and peered into the mail box. There was a letter there. Her body began to shake. She opened the box and picked up the letter with long, trembling fingers. She glanced at the large, square letters with their familiar flourishes. Her heart throbbed painfully. It was Farid's writing . . . Dream or reality? She saw the stairs, the door and the mail box. She put out a trembling hand to touch it. Yes, it was there, it was tangible. She fingered the letter. It was real paper with a thickness and density of its own. She put her fingers to her eyelids. They were open.

She turned the letter over, examining the corners and edges. There was nothing on it other than her name and address. She put it to her nose and met that distinctive smell of paper and postage stamp. She opened the envelope and took out a long sheet of paper, covered with writing:

Fouada . . .

How many days have passed since our last meeting, since that short night that bore the first winds of winter. You were sitting before me, the Nile behind you, in your eyes that strange glint which said: 'I have something new' and your slender fingers drumming on the table with a quiet that hid the volcano beneath. You were silent and I knew you were in pain. After a long silence

112

you said: 'What do you think, Farid? Shall I leave the Ministry?' I understood you. At that moment, you wanted me to say: 'Yes, leave it, come with me.' But, you remember, I said nothing. I always felt that your role was different to mine. Your role is to create something new if you're given the chance, whereas my role is to create the chance for people to create something new. And what is new? Changing the old? And what does change create? Isn't it thought? Do you remember that small child who did the rounds of the tables in the restaurants? Do you remember his wrinkled hand when he held it out for a piece of bread or a piastre? People pitied him and gave him a piastre without thinking. If only they thought about what a piastre does! If only they thought why he was hungry! Yes, Fouada, it's thought, the idea that emerges from the head. Does an idea emerge from the head without expression?

Your role is to create the idea and mine to create the expression. Alone, I can do nothing. My role is neither as easy nor as convincing as the words appear to be. It's a sort of madness, for how do stifled, muted mouths express themselves? How can a voice penetrate through dense, stone walls? It's a sort of madness, but the madness of one individual can create nothing, only collective madness . . . Do you remember that old conversation?

All right, I am not alone. There are others with me. All we have is that simple, dangerous role, and those simple, natural words which were born with the first human . . . to think and to express. Nothing except these words for us to say and write. No cannons or rifles or bombs. Only words.

After we separated that short night, I walked alone down Nile Street, thinking about you, feeling you were in pain, that deep inside you a new idea was struggling to come out, fighting alone against a high wall . . . in the Ministry, at home, in the street and in your skull. Yes, Fouada, there's another wall in your head, one you were not born with, but which day by day was erected out of long silence. I said to myself that night as I walked: 'It is only a short wall, it will collapse finally, when the other walls collapse.'

I did not reach home. A man stood in my way. I think he

was not alone, there were others, perhaps many, all armed. I had nothing. You remember, I was wearing a brown shirt and trousers. They searched my pockets and found nothing. Are words put in a pocket? They grabbed me and put me in irons, but the words were carried in the wind. Can they catch the wind and put it in irons?

The walls surround me, but you are with me. I feel your small, soft hand on my face and see your green eyes looking into mine, that imprisoned, new thing appearing in them that wants to be born but cannot. Do not grieve, Fouada, and do not weep. The words are in the wind beyond the walls, alive and entering hearts with the very air. A day will surely come when the walls will fall and voices will once again be freed to speak.

Farid

WOMAN AT POINT ZERO

'A dramatic symbolised version of female revolt against the norms of the Arab world'
Guardian

'Saadawi tells this story with the nakedness of truth, passion and pain. Her prose is simple, but sharp and enfuriating. *Woman at Point Zero* is the story of one Arab woman, but it reads as if it is every woman's life.'
Spare Rib

'Scorching'
New Internationalist

'Behind the story lies a major radical and feminist analysis of women's oppression, not only in the Arab world or the Third World, but the world over.'
Connexions

'*Woman at Point Zero* should begin the long march towards a realistic and sympathetic portrayal of Arab women and Arab women writers.'
Middle East International

'This bestseller . . . turns a savage eye on not only "kings, princes and rulers", husbands, fathers and lovers, but on their God.'
City Limits

'[Cries] out loudly against the prevalent gender and class oppression of contemporary Egypt at a time when few others have had the courage to raise their voices.'
Middle East Report

'Highly readable . . . a potent reminder of the suffering that many have had to endure.'
Afkar

'A powerful indictment of the treatment of women in many parts of the Middle East'
Labour Herald

GOD DIES BY THE NILE

'Nawal El Saadawi writes with directness and passion, transforming the systematic brutalization of peasants and women into powerful allegory'
New York Times Book Review

'A quietly formidable achievement; its understated evocation of tragedy and strength in the face of victimization make it a graceful classic.
Women's Review

'Powerfully political'
Poetry Nation Review

'Nawal El Saadawi's achievement is to lay bare the thin flesh and huge passions of her characters'
West Indian Digest

CIRCLING SONG

'To read this book is like looking into a kaleidoscope: as each new element in the story is added, so a new configuration is formed'
Independent

'Nawal El Saadawi's technique is impressive: at once precise, controlled and hypnotic, even in translation. The style and meaning of the book are one. A song with no beginning and no end, the author tells its universal story'
Everywoman

'This novel is a powerful example of the kind of anger and desperation to which Arab women writers are beginning to give vent'
Choice

'Nawal El Saadawi is a legend in her own time. This is an ambitious work indeed'
American Book Review

'One of Saadawi's most powerful books that we have had the privilege to read in English. Unusual, original and unexpected, it's one of those very rare books which address you in many languages and can take you in many different directions at once'
Spare Rib

Zed Books Ltd

is a publisher whose international and Third World lists span:

- **Women's Studies**
- **Development**
- **Environment**
- **Current Affairs**
- **International Relations**
- **Children's Studies**
- **Labour Studies**
- **Cultural Studies**
- **Human Rights**
- **Indigenous Peoples**
- **Health**

We also specialize in Area Studies where we have extensive lists in African Studies, Asian Studies, Caribbean and Latin American Studies, Middle East Studies, and Pacific Studies.

For further information about books available from Zed Books, please write to: Catalogue Enquiries, Zed Books Ltd, 57 Caledonian Road, London N1 9BU. Our books are available from distributors in many countries (for full details, see our catalogues), including:

In the USA
Humanities Press International, Inc., 171 First Avenue, Atlantic Highlands, New Jersey 07716.
Tel: (201) 872 1441;
Fax: (201) 872 0717.

In Canada
DEC, 229 College Street, Toronto, Ontario M5T 1R4.
Tel: (416) 971 7051.

In Australia
Wild and Woolley Ltd, 16 Darghan Street, Glebe, NSW 2037.

In India
Bibliomania, C-236 Defence Colony, New Delhi 110 024.

In Southern Africa
David Philip Publisher (Pty) Ltd, PO Box 408, Claremont 7735, South Africa.